PROCLAMATION COMMENTARIES

- The New Testament Witnesses for Preaching   Gerhard Krodel, *Editor*

JESUS CHRIST IN MATTHEW, MARK, AND LUKE

Jack Dean Kingsbury

FORTRESS PRESS   Philadelphia, Pennsylvania

Third printing 1988

Library of Congress Cataloging in Publication Data

Kingsbury, Jack Dean.
    Jesus Christ in Matthew, Mark, and Luke.

    (Proclamation commentaries, the New Testament wit-
nesses for preaching)
    Includes index.
    1. Jesus Christ—History of doctrines—Early church,
ca. 30-600. 2. Bible. N.T. Gospels—Criticism, interpretation, etc. I. Title.
BT198.K54   226'.06   80–69755
ISBN 0–8006–0596–9

3813H88   Printed in the United States of America   1-596

To
Hillman Fischer
Manfred Kwiran
Norman Theiss

CONTENTS

EDITOR'S FOREWORD

It has been gratifying over the past few years to observe the enthusiastic reception the Proclamation Commentaries series has been given by a wide range of people, including laypersons, students, pastors, and professors.

It is envisaged that this book will supplement, not replace, the Proclamation volumes on Matthew, Mark, and Luke. It will do so in at least two ways. First, it contains a chapter on the sayings-source "Q," and thus broadens the scope of the entire series. Although there are some scholars who question the existence of Q, most regard it either as an early layer of oral tradition or as a written document that predates the Gospels. In any event, the scholarly discussion of Q has been intense of late and needs to be taken into account in this series.

The second way in which this book will supplement the other volumes on the Gospels is that it will enable the reader to get a better grasp of the similarities and differences that exist among Matthew, Mark, and Luke. In the case of each of these Gospels, the same key topics are held up for scrutiny. They have to do with the accomplishment of each evangelist and with his understanding of the figure and the mission of Jesus, of discipleship, and of salvation. To treat such large topics within the space of a single chapter is, of course, no easy task. The advantage, however, is that the reader gets a sense of how these evangelists agree with, or diverge from, one another in working with materials that are closely related.

Jack Dean Kingsbury, Professor of New Testament at Union Theological Seminary in Virginia, will already be known to most readers because of his volume in this series on Matthew. Internationally recognized for his work on that Gospel he has been asked to write the commentary on Matthew for the Hermeneia series. This book shows that he is an expert of no mean standing in the whole area of synoptic research. At a time when the field of New Testament is noticeably short on studies that provide a survey of synoptic theology, it is not too much to say that this book can serve beautifully as just such a theology of the synoptic Gospels.

GERHARD KRODEL
Lutheran Theological Seminary at Gettysburg

ABBREVIATIONS

AnBib   Analecta biblica

BETL   Bibliotheca ephemeridum theologicarum lovaniensium

BZNW   Beihefte zur *Zeitschrift für die neutestamentliche Wissenschaft*

HTKNT   Herders theologischer Kommentar zum Neuen Testament

NovTSup   Novum Testamentum, Supplements

NTAbh   Neutestamentliche Abhandlungen

SANT   Studien zum Alten und Neuen Testament

SBLDS   Society of Biblical Literature Dissertation Series

SNTSMS   Society for New Testament Studies Monograph Series

StudNeot   Studia neotestamentica, Studia

SUNT   Studien zur Umwelt des Neuen Testaments

TF   *Theologische Forschung*

WMANT   Wissenschaftliche Monographien zum Alten und Neuen Testament

CHAPTER ONE

THE DOCUMENT OF Q

From earliest days, the church has focused on the cross and resurrection as it has proclaimed the salvation that it confesses God has achieved in Jesus Christ. Thus, one ancient formula, which goes back to the very beginnings of Christianity and is preserved in one of Paul's letters, reads "that Christ died for our sins in accordance with the scriptures, that he was buried, that he was raised on the third day in accordance with the scriptures, and that he appeared . . ." (1 Cor. 15:3–5). As for Paul himself, he bluntly declares that it is his determination "to know nothing . . . except Jesus Christ and him crucified" (1 Cor. 2:2); he who "was crucified in weakness," affirms Paul, nevertheless "lives by the power of God" (2 Cor. 13:4). And when one turns to the earliest Gospel, to Mark, one discovers that the entire flow of the story of Jesus is governed by the cross and resurrection (8:31; 9:31; 10:33–34).

Because the "passion kerygma" is so central to early Christian proclamation, scholars have questioned whether there could have arisen within nascent Christianity any theological document of importance that did not, as Mark, highlight the death and resurrection of Jesus. It may be that in Q one has just such a document, for in place of proclaiming the cross, Q lays stress on the imminent return of Jesus Son of man for judgment.

In this chapter, our aim is to explore this peculiar document of Q, if indeed it was a document, and the community from which it has sprung. How are we to think of the Christians of this community? What understanding does Q convey of Jesus, of his mission, of discipleship, and of salvation? Before taking up these questions, however, we should perhaps first consider several introductory matters pertaining to the document itself.[1]

CRITICAL QUESTIONS IN THE LIGHT OF
MODERN RESEARCH

The document of Q comprises, by definition, those non-Marcan materials that Matthew and Luke have in common. Because Q lies hidden in this fashion in Matthew and Luke, scholars have access to it only through the use of a synopsis.[2] The first to devise such a tool was the great German textual critic Johann Jakob Griesbach in 1774. In order to facilitate a comparison of Matthew, Mark, and Luke with one another, Griesbach had the texts of these Gospels printed out in three parallel columns so that, at any given point, one could spot at a glance the similarities and differences among them. It is perhaps no coincidence that it was only after Griesbach had published his synopsis that Johann Gottfried Eichhorn, in 1794, made his discovery of Q.

Although the existence of Q is a relatively modern postulate, one may ask, in retrospect, whether there is any evidence that the Fathers of the ancient church may have known it. On this score, reference has often been made to the following notice that Eusebius attributes in his *Ecclesiastical History* to Papias, who was Bishop of Hierapolis in Asia Minor and who wrote about A.D. 130: "So, then, Matthew compiled the oracles [sayings] in the Hebrew language, and each one interpreted them as he was able" (III. 39. 16). Although it has frequently been asserted that the sayings of Jesus said here to have been compiled by the apostle Matthew are to be identified in some way with the document of Q, such a suggestion must remain purely conjectural. On balance, the case that Q ever existed as an independent document is one that must be made without appeal to the Church Fathers.

How Q came to be so designated makes for interesting reading but is not immediately discernible. The claim is usually made that "Q" stands for the German word *Quelle,* meaning "source."[3] This, however, seems unlikely. Another explanation is that the sign was chosen as a neutral term and goes back to the German scholar Johannes Weiss,[4] who first used it in the early 1890s.

In content, Q is basically made up of a mass of individual, or groups of, sayings of Jesus. These sayings are prophetic, eschatological, and sapiential in nature.[5] They are organized around some few narrative units, such as the story of the temptation (Luke 4:1–13 //

Matt. 4:1–11), the story of the centurion of Capernaum (Luke 7:1–10 // Matt. 8:5–13), John's question and Jesus' answer (Luke 7:18–23 // Matt. 11:2–6), and the Beelzebul controversy (Luke 11:14–23 // Matt. 12:22–30). In Matthew's Gospel, these materials have their place for the most part in several of the great speeches of Jesus (cf. chaps. 5—7; 10; 11; 18; 23; 24—25). By contrast, in Luke's Gospel they can be found scattered throughout two sections in particular: 6:20—7:35 and 9:51—18:14. Thematically, the dominant notes struck in Q have to do with the message of Jesus concerning the kingdom of God, the imminent expectation of the end, the call to forsake all in order to follow Jesus and to continue his ministry, the challenge to a radical observance of the law, and the warning of impending judgment against Israel. By the same token, there are also some familiar gospel materials that are in especially short supply in Q, namely, miracle stories, parables of Jesus, and Jesus' debates with the leaders of Israel.

Although Q may be described in the main as a mass of discourse materials loosely grouped together, there are good reasons for regarding it as a written document and not simply as a stratum of oral tradition.[6] Thus, the correspondence between the texts of Matthew and of Luke in the Q-sections of these Gospels is at times virtually word-for-word.[7] What is more, the incidence of verbal agreement in all parts of Matthew and Luke attributable to Q is likewise apparently high (71%).[8] Again, if Vincent Taylor is correct, even the order of the units in Q can be recovered on the basis of Luke's Gospel.[9] And the circumstance that Matthew and Luke each contain doublets (texts that are presented twice in the same Gospel), whereby it appears that Mark is followed in the one instance but Q in the other, suggests that Q, like Mark, was a source that had assumed written form.

The question of the provenance of Q is one we shall broach in the last section of this chapter. Suffice it to say for purposes of orientation that it seems that Q arose within a Greek-speaking community which was predominantly Jewish Christian and which was active in the northern regions of Palestine around the middle of the first century A.D.

Uncertainty as to length and exact wording are peculiar problems associated with Q. Because the incidence of verbal agreement in the Q-sections of Matthew and Luke is high but not perfect, it is presently not possible to reconstruct the text of Q with complete accuracy. This means, of course, that theological assessments of Q must remain as tentative as the text on which they are based.

The problem of length is even more vexing. One scholar, for example, takes the position that one can find in Matthew and Luke substantially all that Q ever contained.[10] Another contends that about forty percent of Q has been lost.[11] Whatever the truth may be, the difficulty is that since Q is, by definition, said to comprise those non-Marcan materials that Matthew and Luke have in common, it cannot be determined whether there are not portions of "special Matthew" or "special Luke" which should rightfully be consigned to Q. Exegetically, the disadvantage of not knowing the exact limits of Q is obvious, for it renders that much more uncertain the theological evaluation of its contents.

Yet another problem concerns the question as to how accurately the interpreter can chart the development of Q. It seems certain that the materials one finds in Q were gathered over a period of some years. This suggests that they made their way through the hands of successive redactors, or editors. Is it possible for the interpreter to delineate the peculiar shape and thought content that these materials may have assumed at various stages earlier than the one at which Matthew and Luke took them up into their Gospels?

Some students of Q believe that such a delineation is possible and hence distinguish an earlier redaction in Q from a later one.[12] The difficulty, however, is that in so doing they tend to outrun the evidence. Thus, insufficient account is taken of the circumstance that the only basis for determining the redaction of Q is the selection of materials one finds in it and the peculiar composition of the constituent parts. The shape of Q is the result of individual sayings or units having been grouped together by means of "catch-words" or because of subject matter relatedness. Q is without the major summary passages that occur in the synoptic Gospels, which inform the reader of the literary and theological intention of the writer (cf., e.g., Matt. 4:23; 9:35; 11:1); moreover, it possesses a "preferred vocabulary" only to a limited extent. For these reasons, one must be skeptical that the interpreter can achieve certainty as to the "editorial policy" of any given redactor of Q. Not only that, but there is the further difficulty that the interpreter cannot know, with any high degree of precision, the exact wording or length of Q at any given point. Accordingly, in this brief study we shall explore the redaction of Q as it can be recovered from a comparison of Matthew and Luke. It is the "final form" of Q, then, that will occupy us.

Aside from these questions that have to do with the length, the exact wording, and the literary development of Q, there is the additional problem that some scholars dispute the very existence of Q.[13] They do so because they contest the validity of the two-source hypothesis. They believe that it does not explain adequately the relationships, involving similarities and differences, among the three synoptic Gospels. On the contrary, some scholars reason that the so-called Griesbach hypothesis can account better for these relationships, namely, that Matthew's Gospel was written first and that Luke used Matthew and that Mark's Gospel is a popularization of both Matthew and Luke.[14] Thus far, whatever the weaknesses of the two-source hypothesis, it has not been overthrown in the minds of most scholars, and the Griesbach hypothesis has not asserted itself. At the same time, the attack on the two-source hypothesis and therefore on the existence of Q does mean that the basis for research on Q is to this extent more fragile and the results less certain.

To save space, we shall refer to individual passages in this chapter on Q in terms of where they may be found in the Gospel of Luke. The reader who takes a synopsis to hand can easily locate the Matthaean parallel of any given passage. Perhaps the best attempt so far to reconstruct the Greek text of Q is that of Athanasius Polag.[15]

IMMINENT EXPECTATION OF THE END

The one factor that, more than any other, accounts for the theological character of Q—its distinctive understanding of Jesus, of discipleship, and of salvation—is the view it projects of the history of salvation. This view contains elements that derive from both the wisdom and the apocalyptic traditions of Judaism. Throughout history, God, or the Wisdom of God, has continually been sending to Israel prophets and messengers to call his people to repentance (Luke 11:49–51; 13:34). This long line of prophetic messengers embraces, successively, the OT prophets (Luke 11:47, 49–51), John the Baptist (Luke 7:26, 33), and Jesus (Luke 7:34). For his part, Jesus, too, sends his disciples to Israel in continuation of his ministry (Luke 10:3); hence, the disciples take their place in this line of prophetic messengers as well (Luke 6:23). One mark of the scheme of salvation-history as found in Q, therefore, is this strong notion of continuity: John, Jesus, and the disciples follow in the footsteps of the OT prophets.

Highly significant, however, is the nature of this continuity that unites John, Jesus, and the disciples with the OT prophets. It is a continuity, not of acceptance, but of repudiation. Israel has not received the OT prophets, John, Jesus, or the disciples. It has killed the prophets (Luke 11:49–51; 13:34), accused John of being possessed of a demon (Luke 7:33), charged Jesus with being a glutton and a drunkard, a friend of tax-collectors and sinners (Luke 7:34), and persecuted the disciples (Luke 6:22–23). Hence, the history of salvation as Q describes it has virtually become a history of judgment against Israel.

Nevertheless, the die on Israel has not yet been cast. Even so, time is running out. History has already moved into its final phase. The OT prophets and John belong to the "time of the law and the prophets" (Luke 16:16). Jesus and his disciples belong to the time of fulfillment (Luke 7:22; 10:23–24). For its part, the time of fulfillment is the "time of the eschatological harvest" (Luke 10:2). In sum, therefore, the scheme of salvation history as found in Q conveys a strong sense of both hope and urgency: a sense of hope because it may be that Israel will yet hear the word of God's messengers and turn to God in repentance; a sense of urgency because history, and with it God's forbearance, is rapidly approaching its end.

We stated that, in the perspective of Q, John belongs to the "time of the law and the prophets" and that Jesus and the disciples belong to the "time of the eschatological harvest." How, then, does John relate to Jesus?

Q distinguishes between the OT prophets and John on the one hand and between John and Jesus on the other. It does so on the basis of the different roles these figures play within God's plan of salvation. Compared with the OT prophets, for example, John is not only a prophet but "more than a prophet" (Luke 7:26). In what sense? In the sense that he is God's special messenger sent to ready Israel for the coming of the Mightier One and the impending end-time judgment (Luke 3:16–17; 7:27). As God's special messenger, John himself comes in fulfillment of OT prophecy and thus is an end-time figure (Luke 7:27; Mal. 3:1). Consequently, he stands on the boundary between the two epochs of the "law and the prophets" and of the "eschatological harvest": he brings the one to a close and prepares the way for the other. By contrast, Jesus is that Mightier One toward whom John points (Luke 3:16; 7:18–19, 22–23). He is the Son of man, God's supreme messenger in the history of salvation (Luke 7:33–35). With his coming, the time of the eschatological harvest, which is at the end of time, commences.

It is plain from the preceding that the concept of salvation history in Q is strongly oriented toward the end-phase of history. This orientation, in turn, reveals what is central to this concept: the notion of the imminent expectation of the end. In Q, history is seen as hastening toward its consummation, and when it has run its course Jesus, the transcendent Son of man, will suddenly appear from heaven to carry out the eschatological judgment.

But as dominant as the imminent expectation of the end is in Q, one should not on this account assume that Q is simply one-dimensional and without nuance in its approach to eschatology. On the contrary, there is at least one clear indication of the awareness that if the parousia of the Son of man is a thing of the near future, it may not be wholly immediate. In the parable of the faithful and prudent slave, the slave is depicted as saying in his heart, "My Lord is delayed in coming . . ." (Luke 12:45). As Q portrays it the paradox holds true: the end is imminent, but still there is time.

THE FIGURE OF JESUS

Q begins with the preaching of John the Baptist against Israel (Luke 3:2–4, 7–9, 16–17). In his preaching, John designates Jesus as the "Mightier One," the mediator of salvation or damnation (Luke 3:16). In Mark's Gospel, the designation "Mightier One" characterizes Jesus as the royal Messiah, or Christ (1:1, 7). But Q never once refers to Jesus as "Messiah." Nonetheless, in Q, too, Jesus is the decisive figure in the history of salvation. From the time of his appearance in Israel, present and future stand under his aegis. To indicate this, Q speaks of Jesus both as the Son of man who will come and as the agent of God who has come.

Jesus as the Son of Man Who Will Come

Correlative to the belief that the end is imminent is belief in Jesus as the transcendent "Son of man." As the one who is eagerly awaited, Jesus Son of man is the "coming one" (Luke 3:16; 7:17; 13:35). As the one who is invested with absolute authority, he is the "mightier one" (Luke 3:16). And as the one whom his followers serve, he is the "Lord" (Luke 12:42–46; 13:25–27; 19:12–26).

Q is vivid in its portrayal of the parousia of Jesus Son of man. At the end of time, he will be revealed from heaven in the sight of all (Luke 17:26–30). His revelation will be instantaneous, like lightning that flashes and lights up the sky from one side to the other (Luke 17:24). His sudden appearance will also catch people unawares, as did the deluge at the time of Noah (Luke 17:26–27). It is furthermore an event that one who is irresolute will not survive: in the face of it, only the individual who is prepared to relinquish everything he possesses, including his life, will persevere (Luke 17:31–33). And it is an event that will result in the radical separation of people: two women will be grinding grain together; the one will be taken and hence saved, but the other will be left and so abandoned to her fate (Luke 17:34–35).

Judgment is the purpose for which Jesus Son of man will come (Luke 3:16–17). The "good news" he has proclaimed while on earth and the "powerful acts" he has performed are harbingers of his coming (Luke 7:19, 22). In addition, his coming for judgment will likewise mark the inauguration in splendor of the consummated kingdom of God (Luke 13:18–19, 20–21, 28–29; 22:20). Also, from the final judgment itself there will be no immunity, neither for Israel nor for Jesus' followers. As things stand, Israel will most assuredly incur condemnation, for it has heard the preaching of Jesus but has refused to repent (Luke 11:29–32) and has persecuted those who continue in his stead (Luke 13:34–35). By contrast, even Gentiles will be admitted to the kingdom, where they will "sit at table" with the patriarchs and prophets of OT times (Luke 13:28–

30). As for the followers of Jesus, they must keep themselves in a state of "readiness" if they are to persevere in the judgment (Luke 12:40). This means that they will "confess" Jesus before people (Luke 12:8) and be "good," "wise," and "faithful" in his service (Luke 12:42–44; 19:12–26). Otherwise, should they "deny" Jesus before people (Luke 12:9) or prove themselves to be "workers of iniquity" (Luke 13:27), they, like all the wicked, will be consigned by the Son of man to punishment (Luke 12:45–46; 19:20–26).

Jesus as the Agent of God Who Has Come

But Jesus is not only the transcendent Son of man who will come; he is also the agent of God who has come. The earthly Jesus is the bearer in Q of two separate titles. When it is a matter of his personal relationship to the Father, he is described as "the Son," or the "Son of God" (Luke 4:1–13; 10:22). When it is a matter of the mission in Israel for which God has sent him, he is described, again, as the "Son of man" (Luke 7:34; 9:58; 12:10).

Unlike the synoptic Gospels, Q has no story of the baptism of Jesus. In Mark, the function of the story of the baptism is to present Jesus to the reader as the royal Son of God whom God has endowed with divine authority (the Spirit) and chosen for messianic ministry (1:10–11). The title "Son of God" in Mark is a further definition of "Messiah" (cf. 1:1, 11; 14:61).

Q differs from Mark in that it does not associate the terms "the Son" or the "Son of God" with the title of "Messiah." Still, Q contains a pericope that functions in the same manner in it as the baptism does in Mark. This pericope is Jesus' thanksgiving to the Father (Luke 10:21–22). It revolves around the exclusive relationship that exists between Jesus the Son and God his Father. The Father has entrusted Jesus, the Son, with "all things," thus endowing him with divine authority (Luke 10:22; cf. 11:20). Moreover, the Father "knows" the Son (Luke 10:22), i.e., the Son is the one whom the Father has chosen and sent on his mission of word and deed to Israel (Luke 10:16; cf. 7:22). By the same token, the Son "knows" the Father (Luke 10:22), i.e., the Son is of one will with the Father and the one through whom the Father reveals himself and his divine purposes to human beings (Luke 10:21–22). In short, therefore, the claim this passage makes is that the Son stands forth in the world as the unique agent of God and hence as the one through whom God effects salvation.

The story of the temptation of Jesus (Luke 4:1–13) may be treated in Q as something of a commentary on this pericope on Jesus' thanksgiving to the Father. The order in which Matthew has arranged the three "tests" is perhaps the more original. Once again Jesus appears as the Son of God (Luke 4:3, 9). He is the antitype to Israel of old, which was also God's son (Exod. 4:22–23). What is at stake in Jesus' confrontations with the devil is precisely his exclusive relationship to God his Father. The fact that the Spirit leads him into the desert is a reminder that he is a figure of divine authority (Luke 4:1).

In the first temptation, the devil bids Jesus to use his authority as the Son of God to convert a stone into bread (Luke 4:3). Were Jesus to do this, however, he would be "forcibly" altering the circumstances into which God has brought him. In satisfying his hunger, he would be doing his own will instead of submitting himself to what God has willed for him. This was the sin into which Israel fell in its wilderness wanderings when, in hunger, it murmured against God (Deut. 8:2–3; Exod. 16:2–4). But Jesus Son of God is of one will with the Father. It is for him to serve the Father and not to serve himself. Accordingly, he resists the devil's suggestion that he use his divine authority to his own advantage with the words, "It is written, 'Man shall not live by bread alone' " (Luke 4:4).

In the second temptation, the devil invites Jesus Son of God to put his unique relationship to God to the test (Luke 4:9–12). By casting himself down from the temple, Jesus could give God the opportunity to prove that he will make good on his promise in scripture to protect Jesus from harm in time of danger (cf. Ps. 91:11–12). At Massah, Israel of old tested God in similar fashion: the thirsty people demanded of Moses that God demonstrate that he is with them by giving them water to drink (Deut. 6:16; Exod. 17:1–7). But Jesus Son of God "knows" the Father. Consequently, he knows that it is manifestly not God's will that he "test out" God's faithfulness to his promises by jumping from the temple into the arms of angels. Hence, Jesus rejects the devil's proposal with the words, "It is said, 'You shall not tempt the Lord your God' " (Luke 4:12).

In the third temptation, the devil shows Jesus "in a moment of time" all the kingdoms of the world (Luke 4:5–8). He offers to give Jesus authority, or rule, over them if only he will worship him. In Canaan, Israel succumbed to the lure of false gods; it "went after" the gods of the people round about it (Deut. 6:14). But again, Jesus Son of God "knows" the Father. It is the Father, not the devil, who is the "Lord of heaven and earth" (Luke 10:21). It is the Father alone, therefore, to whom worship is due, and it is from him that Jesus derives the divine authority that is his (Luke 10:22). In view of this, Jesus replies to the devil, "It is written, 'You shall worship the Lord your God, and him only shall you serve' " (Luke 4:8).

In Q, then, no less than in Mark, Jesus embarks upon his ministry to Israel as a figure of divine authority. As the agent of God, he both knows and does the Father's will. Where Israel of old failed in its tests of obedience, he does not. As a result, it is he and he alone through whom the Father reveals himself to people.

THE MISSION OF JESUS

Jesus is preceded in Q by John the Baptist (Luke 7:33–34). If in Mark's Gospel John is identified as Elijah redivivus, in Q he is less specifically described, as we have noted, as a "prophet" who is also "more than a prophet" (Luke 7:26). John is more than a prophet because he is the special messenger God has sent to prepare the way for Jesus (Luke 7:27). Hence, in Q, too, John may be said to be the forerunner of Jesus.

But it is as the forerunner of Jesus, the transcendent Son of man and end-time Judge, that John first appears in Q. In the preaching with which Q begins, John announces: "But he who is mightier than I is coming . . . ; his winnowing fork is in his hand and he will clear his threshing floor, and he will gather the wheat into his granary, but the chaff he will burn with unquenchable fire!" (Luke 3:16–17).

In a later passage in Q, however, this "thoroughgoing apocalyptic" of John's opening words is modified to the extent that John is also portrayed as the forerunner of Jesus, the earthly Son of man. Thus, through the agency of his disciples John himself puts the question to Jesus, "Are you he who is to come?" (Luke 7:19). In his reply to John, Jesus makes reference, significantly, not to the latter-day judgment but to the words and deeds which typify his earthly ministry to Israel ("Go and tell John what you see and hear" [Luke 7:22]).

John, then, is the forerunner both of Jesus, the earthly Son of man, and of Jesus, the transcendent Son of man. Still, the emphasis in Q, by virtue of the arrangement of these two passages, is on John as the forerunner of Jesus, the transcendent Son of man. Hence, to grasp the distinctive picture Q paints of John in his relationship to Jesus, John must be seen to be the forerunner of Jesus, the earthly Son of man, whose ministry of word and deed presages already his imminent coming as the transcendent Son of man and apocalyptic Judge.

The ministry John performs in Israel is one of preparation (Luke 3:2–4, 7–9, 16–17; 7:27). His preaching is, as we know, replete with the imagery of Jewish apocalyptic: he proclaims the eschatological judgment and the imminent end of history. The wrath of divine judgment, cries John, is already near at hand (Luke 3:7). Already the ax of God's retribution lies at the root of the trees (Luke 3:9). Already the Mightier One, the eschatological Judge, stands with his winnowing fork poised, prepared to separate the wheat from the chaff (Luke 3:17). In the face of such eschatological judgment, descendency from Abraham, with its alleged merit, counts for nothing (Luke 3:8). Nevertheless, even at this late hour all is not lost and there is a way of escape. What each Israelite must do is to repent, to turn to God, and to lead the new life of obedience to his will which such repentance engenders (Luke 3:8). By so doing, the individual can persevere in the final judgment and flee the hell of fire (Luke 3:17).

Whereas John is almost singularly a preacher of judgment, Jesus not only announces judgment but proffers salvation as well (Luke 7:22; 11:32). The focus of Jesus' ministry, like that of John, is on Israel (Luke 7:31–35; 13:34–35). Although the name "Galilee" does not occur in Q, this is the region that seems to be presupposed as the setting for Jesus' activity. Indication of this is the fact that Jesus enjoins his disciples to summon such cities of Galilee as "Chorazin," "Bethsaida,"[16] and "Capernaum" to repentance (Luke 10:13–16).

Because Q is basically made up of sayings of Jesus and is not of the same genre as the canonical Gospels,[17] it has no itinerary that sketches the movement of Jesus. Vague though these details are, the synoptic Gospels nonetheless picture Jesus as being in a "synagogue" or "house," in or near a "city" or "village," on the "Sea of Galilee" or "beside the sea," or on a "mountain" or "on the way." Q contains virtually no such references (but cf. Luke 9:5; 10:11–12). And by the same token, neither does Q identify, except in rare instances (cf., e.g., Luke 11:39, 42), the audience Jesus is addressing with his respective sayings. The latter feature, however, poses no real problem, for the audience of Jesus can readily be inferred from the form and content of his sayings.

On the other hand, what Q does make clear is that Jesus carries out his ministry in Israel among the common people, or the largely disenfranchised, and the outcasts of society. In the beatitudes, for example, Jesus promises to the "poor" the eschatological kingdom (Luke 6:20) and to the "hungry" participation in the messianic banquet (Luke 6:21). As for his disciples, Jesus refers to them as "infants" (Luke 10:21) and as "little ones" (Luke 17:2), thus contrasting them in the one case with the "wise and understanding" in Israel and in the other with the arrogant and willful who would cause them to stumble in their faith or to lose it. In other respects, Jesus himself bears the stigma of being the "friend of tax-collectors and sinners" (Luke 7:34). Apparently, it is they for whom the "lost sheep" stands as a symbol in the parable (Luke 15:4–7).

The ministry Jesus undertakes among the common people and the outcasts of Israel consists of preaching and healing (Luke 7:22; 10:24). Given the circumstance that Q is a sayings-source, it reveals by its very composition that it is the words of Jesus which are at the heart of what he intends. Consequently, we turn first to Jesus' ministry of preaching and teaching.

Jesus' Ministry of Preaching and Teaching

Jesus' ministry of the word picks up in Q on John's preaching of the imminent end of all things. As Q portrays it, Jesus, the supreme agent of God, proclaims in Israel the eschatological kingdom, declares the will of God, and gives instructions to his followers.

In Jesus' initial words of proclamation in Q, the dominant theme is the kingdom of God (Luke 6:20–23). In biblical tradition, the kingdom of God has to do with the sovereignty of God, his reign over all creation (Exod. 15:18; Pss. 47:2; 93:1–2; 96:10; 99:1–5; 103:19). A good paraphrase of it is the "rule of God." In Q as in other early Christian documents, the view obtains that when Jesus, the transcendent Son of man, shall usher in the consummated kingdom at the final judgment, the suzerainty of God over all things will suddenly become manifest to the whole of humankind (cf. Luke 13:18–19, 20–21, 28–29; 17:26–27, 30). For those who are the disciples of Jesus Son of man, this coming of God's kingdom in splendor will mean salvation. It is, therefore, the object of both their hope and their prayers. As Jesus himself has taught them, they petition God: "Father, . . . let your kingdom come!" (Luke 11:2).

If the kingdom of God is a future reality in Q, it is a present reality as well, perceptible to the "eyes of faith." In the words and deeds of Jesus, the agent of God and the earthly Son of man, one encounters the kingdom even now (Luke 11:20). In the beatitude he addresses to his disciples, Jesus himself puts it this way: "Blessed are the eyes which see the things which you see! For I tell you that many prophets and kings desired to see the things which you see, and did not see them, and to hear the things which you hear, and did not hear them" (Luke 10:23–24).

As the bearer of God's kingdom, the earthly Jesus summons people through his words and deeds to repentance and to faith (Luke 7:22–23; 11:32). In so doing, he likewise summons them to discipleship and thus to a life that is carried out in the sphere of God's end-time kingdom (Luke 6:20–22; 9:59–62; 10:23–24). To live in the sphere of the end-time kingdom, however, is to have escaped from the sphere of Satan's kingdom (11:17–20); for Satan is also one who rules in the sense that he, too, exercises authority over all who do his will (Luke 4:1–13; 11:18). Accordingly, called to decision by Jesus, people either enter the sphere of God's gracious rule or they reject Jesus' call and refuse to enter (Luke 7:22–23; 11:23, 31–32). But either way, the decision they have made is of ultimate consequence, because the final judgment will see it ratified (Luke 12:8–9).

In the twin kingdom parables of the mustard seed and of the leaven (Luke 13:18–19, 20–21), the Jesus of Q "summarizes" in pictorial speech his proclamation about the kingdom of God. In the first parable, the tiny "mustard seed" grows until, miraculously, it becomes a "tree." In the second parable, the little lump of "yeast" causes the dough to swell until the "whole" mass has become fully leavened. The tiny "mustard seed" and the little lump of "leaven" allude to the small beginnings of the kingdom as reflected in the ministry of Jesus (and of his followers). The "tree" and the "whole" mass of leavened bread allude to the magnificent, consummated kingdom of God that the Son of man will unveil at his final, sudden appearance from heaven. Two things to note in these parables are that there is continuity in each between the inconsiderable beginnings and the great end, and that the end constitutes the culmination of the entire process of growth that has been sketched. In addition, this process of growth is described as taking place rapidly. In the thought of Q, these parabolic features translate themselves into the claim that it is from the seemingly insignificant beginnings of the ministry of Jesus (and of his followers) that the magnificent kingdom of God, the culmination of all history, will, at the sudden appearance of the Son of man in the immediate future, most assuredly issue.

Another major aspect of Jesus' ministry of the word in Q is his teaching concerning the will of God. As teacher of the will of God, Jesus is at the same time the authoritative interpreter of the law of Moses. But although Jesus interprets Moses, he is not presented as pitting himself against Moses. It is noteworthy, for example, that the Jesus of Q does not avail himself of the antithetic formula so typical of Matthew: "You have heard that it was said [by Moses] to the men of old . . . but I say to you" (cf., e.g., Matt. 5:21, 33). On the contrary, Jesus is envisaged in Q as upholding the law of Moses. With no hint of a disclaimer, he flatly asserts: "Until heaven and earth pass away, not one serif shall pass away from the law!" (Luke 16:17).

Still, it is also the case in Q that Jesus reinterprets the law in more stringent terms. Thus, Deut. 24:1–4 sanctions divorce, but Jesus says: "Every one who divorces his wife and marries another commits adultery, and whoever marries a woman divorced from her husband commits adultery" (Luke 16:18). Again, the law permits and even enjoins in some cases acts of retribution (cf. Exod. 21:23–25; Lev. 24:19–20; Deut. 19:21); by contrast, Jesus strongly forbids all such acts (Luke 6:29–30). And although the law commands love of the neighbor, i.e., love of the "sons of your own people" (Lev. 19:18), Jesus places this command in a totally new light by calling for love of one's enemies as well (Luke 6:27–28, 35).

But this, of course, raises a question: Is it not contradictory to claim that Jesus both upholds the Mosaic law in Q and yet reinterprets it, even to the point of "revising" it? The answer is that the contradiction is only apparent. It is so because the purpose of Jesus' reinterpretation of the law in Q is not to abrogate the commands of Moses, but to bring out their true intention. What this true intention is is stated by Jesus in sayings such as these: "Be merciful, even as your Father is merciful" (Luke 6:36); and, "As you wish that men would do to you, so you also do to them" (Luke 6:31). In other words, the ground of the law in Q, and indeed of the whole of God's will, is that quality of love that takes its cue from God himself.

More striking than Jesus' interpretation of the Mosaic law in Q is his treatment of the Pharisaic tradition of the elders.[18] This is the oral code with which contemporary Phariseeism supplemented the written law of Moses. Even though Jesus denounces the Pharisees and their scribes in a series of seven woes, or execrations (Luke 11:39–52), there is no clear sign that he fundamentally sets their oral code aside. In his first woe against the Pharisees, for instance, Jesus does not challenge but tacitly acknowledges the validity of their regulations governing the cleansing of cup and dish (Luke 11:39–41). Similarly, he states in the second woe with respect to the Pharisaic stipulations concerning the tithing of herbs that these ought "not to be neglected" (Luke 11:42). And in his final woe, he seems to presuppose that the Pharisaic lawyers, or scribes, do in fact possess the authority to teach in Israel (Luke 11:52).

Hence, it is not the tradition of the elders per se to which the Jesus of Q objects. Instead, he condemns the Pharisees because their understanding and observance of this tradition are such as to be at odds with the deepest intention of the will of God, namely, the exercise of love (Luke 6:31, 36). The upshot is that Jesus pronounces eschatological judgment upon the Pharisees or their scribes for all of the following. They occupy themselves with minor things, such as the regulations pertaining to the cleansing of vessels, but overlook completely the perversity of their lives (Luke 11:39). They go beyond what the law requires and tithe the most insignificant of the garden herbs, but in the process they neglect those matters that are of the very essence of the law (Luke 11:42). They are vain and vie with one another simply for status in the public eye (Luke 11:43). They are like unmarked tombs people unwittingly step on, defiling those who come into contact with them without their even knowing it (Luke 11:44). They weigh people down with heavy burdens of religious observances, but do nothing to assist them as they struggle to keep these observances (Luke 11:46). Although they seemingly honor the prophets, in reality they are as their fathers, who refused the message of the prophets and shed their blood (Luke 11:47–48). And instead of using their status as the teachers of Israel to lead people to an understanding of God and his will for them, they have used it to thwart such understanding (Luke 11:52). In sum, therefore, Jesus' polemic against the Pharisees and their scribes in Q is that neither their lives nor their views on the law comport themselves with the will of God.

A third major aspect of Jesus' ministry of the word in Q is the instructions he gives his followers. This aspect, however, we shall consider later, as we discuss the topic of discipleship.

Jesus' Ministry of Healing

Compared with the synoptic Gospels, Q devotes remarkably little space to the healing ministry of Jesus. In all, Q contains only the following: one summary passage, in which Jesus calls attention to the fact that he restores to health the blind, the lame, lepers, and the deaf, and raises to life the dead (Luke 7:22); two accounts of healings, in which he cures a centurion's slave and casts out a demon (Luke 7:1–10; 11:14); and the debate he has with the Jews over whether, in exorcising demons, he is in collusion with Beelzebul, the prince of demons (Luke 11:15, 17–22).

But despite this meager fund, the significance that Q attaches to the healings of Jesus is plain to see. They mark the fulfillment of OT prophecy (cf. Isa. 29:18–19; 35:5–6; 61:1), and thus point both to the presence of God's kingdom in Jesus' earthly ministry and to its glorious appearance in the near future when he, the Son of man, will be revealed from heaven (Luke 7:19, 22–23; cf. 3:16–17).

As a sign of the presence of God's kingdom this side of the parousia, the healings of Jesus attest to the overthrow of Satan. This is the import of the Beelzebul controversy (Luke 11:14–15, 17–22). Jesus exorcises a demon from a dumb man and he speaks. This elicits the charge from some of the bystanders that he has accomplished this act by invoking the power of Beelzebul. Jesus' reply is to the effect that this charge makes little sense, because Satan would then be waging war with himself. On the contrary, the truth of the matter is that in freeing people from the bondage of demonic possession, he is in reality removing them from the sphere of Satan's influence and bringing them into the gracious sphere of the kingdom of God. He is, in short, "depopulating" Satan's kingdom and hence bringing him to fall.

The function of Jesus' healings in Q is basically not different from that of his preaching. They call Israel to repentance and impel all who witness them to the decision of faith or of unfaith. The question they pose is this: Is Jesus, or is he not, the eschatological agent of God in whom one encounters even now the kingdom of God which is soon to be unveiled in splendor (Luke 7:22–23; 11:20; cf. 10: 13)? On the individual's answer to this question hangs his ultimate fate.

Israel's Repudiation of Jesus

Israel is most often referred to in Q as "this generation" (Luke 7:31; 11:29, 31, 32, 51).[19] This term is one of disapprobation and occurs in sayings that bespeak judgment upon Israel. Thus, the very use of the term is indicative in Q of Israel's repudiation of Jesus.

In the perspective of Q, John the Baptist and Jesus stand in the long line of prophets and messengers that God, or the Wisdom of God, has continually sent to Israel (Luke 7:33–35; 11:49–51). Like those before them, John and Jesus, too, have summoned Israel to repentance: John by his preaching and baptism (Luke 3:3, 7–9), and Jesus by his preaching and powerful acts (Luke 7:22–23; 11: 32). For his part, however, Jesus has surpassed his predecessors, for with him the time of the eschatological harvest has begun: in summoning Israel to repentance, Jesus has likewise summoned it to discipleship and to life in the sphere of God's end-time Rule. In the imagery of Q, Jesus has looked to gather Israel "as a hen gathers her brood under her wings" (Luke 13:34).

But the result has always been the same. In times past, Israel has killed, persecuted, and stoned the prophets and messengers sent to it (Luke 11:47–48, 50–51; 13:34). Confronted by John's proclamation, it has made false appeal to its descendancy from Abraham (Luke 3:8) or has dismissed John as one who has a demon (Luke

7:33). Toward Jesus, the response has been more virulent. Israel has demanded that he prove, by means of a sign of unmistakably divine origin, that his ministry has been authorized by God (Luke 11:16, 29). It has cast aspersions on his fidelity to the law and the will of God by decrying him as a "glutton and a drunkard, a friend of tax-collectors and sinners" (Luke 7:34). It has charged him with being in consort with Beelzebul, the prince of demons (Luke 11:15). And it has failed to recognize that in Jesus' ministry of the word "something greater" is being proclaimed than either the wisdom of Solomon or the preaching of Jonah, namely, Jesus' message of the kingdom (Luke 11:31–32).

As a result of its repudiation of Jesus, Israel can expect to incur certain judgment at the end of the age, which is even now approaching (Luke 11:31–32). Already the earthly Son of man has left Jerusalem and God has deserted the temple, leaving it ripe for catastrophe (Luke 13:35). Israel's next encounter with Jesus will be on the final day of retribution, when he will be revealed as the transcendent Son of man (Luke 13:35). On that day, contemporary Israel will be held responsible for the blood of all the prophets from every age (Luke 11:50–51). Indeed, so great is its guilt that it will be "more tolerable" on that day for the pagan cities of Tyre and Sidon than for the people of the Galilean cities of Chorazin, Bethsaida, and Capernaum (Luke 10:13–15). In point of fact, with the appearance of the kingdom at the end of history, even Gentiles will come from the four regions of the world and recline at the messianic table with the patriarchs and prophets (Luke 13:28–29). Israel, on the other hand, will be "thrust out" and relegated to the place of·extreme torment (Luke 13:28).

DISCIPLESHIP

Although Israel as a whole has not received Jesus, he has nonetheless gathered a circle of adherents about him. These adherents are those who have heard his summons to repentance and have joined themselves to him (Luke 7:23; 11:23, 32).

The terms by which the adherents of Jesus are known in Q characterize them further. Interestingly, they are not designated as "the twelve" (but cf. Luke 22:30) but as "brothers" of one another

(Luke 6:41–42; 17:3). Through the call of Jesus, they have become "sons of God" (Luke 6:35), and God has become their "Father" (Luke 6:36; 11:2, 13; 12:30). They have likewise become the "disciples" of Jesus (Luke 6:40; 14:26–27), for they "follow" after him (Luke 9:57–60; 14:27) and serve him as "slaves" serve their lord (Luke 12:42–46; 19:12–26).

As those who have heard the summons of Jesus and joined themselves to him, the disciples in Q conduct their lives in the sphere of God's end-time kingdom (Luke 6:20–23; 10:23–24; 13:18–21). As the recipients of God's favor in Jesus, they in turn "seek first his [God's] kingdom" (Luke 12:31), which is to say that they devote themselves totally to the doing of God's will as taught by Jesus. In the words of Jesus himself, "No one is able to serve two masters . . . God and mammon" (Luke 16:13); what the disciples must be about is having "treasure in heaven," because "where your treasure is, there will your heart be also" (Luke 12:33–34). Indeed, such concentration on the things of God is all the more imperative in view of the circumstance that already the moment is fast approaching when God will suddenly grant the petition for which the disciples pray, ". . . your kingdom come!" (Luke 11:2).

Accordingly, the disciples of Jesus are presented in Q as giving themselves without reserve to the affairs of the kingdom in the sure confidence of its imminent appearance in splendor. Such devotion commits the disciples, in emulation of Jesus, to a style of life that has been dubbed "itinerant radicalism." What is the peculiar nature of this style of life?

Itinerant Radicalism

The notion of itinerant radicalism[20] is grounded in Q in this word of Jesus: "A disciple is not above his teacher, but every one when he is fully taught will be like his teacher" (Luke 6:40). To be like Jesus in Q means, among other things, that the disciples forgo domicile, family, and possessions.

To forgo domicile in Q is to renounce the security of home and institution and to endure the vagaries of itinerancy. "Foxes have holes, and birds of the air have nests," but the disciples, in imitation of Jesus Son of man, have "nowhere to lay [their] head[s]" (Luke

9:58). In commissioning the disciples to their ministry, Jesus instructs them: "Go your way; behold, I send you out as lambs in the midst of wolves" (Luke 10:3).

But discipleship furthermore demands of the followers of Jesus in Q that they surrender their ties to family and relatives. Jesus makes this point in what seem to be two of his harshest sayings: "If any one comes to me and does not hate father and mother and son and daughter, he cannot be my disciple" (cf. Luke 14:26 and Matt. 10: 37); and again, "Do you think that I have come to give peace on earth? No, I tell you, but rather division; for henceforth in one house there will be five divided, three against two and two against three; they will be divided, father against son and son against father, mother against daughter and daughter against her mother, mother-in-law against her daughter-in-law and daughter-in-law against her mother-in-law" (Luke 12:51–53).

Finally, the disciples in Q are also called to a life that shuns the amassing of worldly goods. In one passage, Jesus enjoins his followers: "Therefore I tell you, do not be anxious about your life, what you shall eat, nor about your body, what you shall put on" (Luke 12:22). And in another passage he commands: "Sell your possessions, and give alms . . ." (Luke 12:33).

The picture Q sketches of the disciples, therefore, is that of a group of followers whom Jesus has summoned away from home, family, and possessions so that they might, in emulation of his style of life, wander from place to place in his service and in the service of the kingdom. This group of followers constitutes a new community within Israel. It is the community of the end-time, which is guided by the words of Jesus and which lives in total dependence upon the providence of God. Toward one another and toward all others, this community practices the ethic of love, even as Jesus has enunciated it: "Be merciful, even as your Father is merciful . . . [for] as you wish that men would do to you, so you also do to them" (Luke 6:31, 36).

Continuing the Ministry of Jesus

Jesus commissions the disciples in Q to continue his ministry in Israel.[21] Their time, like his, is also the "time of the eschatological harvest" (Luke 10:2). They are his "apostles," authorized by him to act on his authority and in his stead (Luke 10:3, 16). He has given them insight into the mystery of his person and into the way in which God is working out his saving purposes in these final days (Luke 10:21-24).

Thus, indicative of the ministry of the disciples in Q is a strong sense of urgency. They do as Jesus has done, namely, summon Israel to repentance and to discipleship in view of the end-time judgment, which is imminent (Luke 10:13-16). Because of the imminence of the judgment, haste is the order of the day, and so they "greet no one on the way" (Luke 10:4; cf. 2 Kings 4:29) and "do not go from house to house" when once they have found quarters in any village (Luke 10:7).

The disciples, in moving from place to place in Israel, announce the nearness of God's eschatological kingdom and heal the sick (Luke 10:8-9). To attest to their mission with their outward appearance and to disassociate themselves from the leadership of Israel and the rich, they take with them on their journeys neither the simplest of weapons, the staff, nor such needful items as the money-bag, the knapsack, or even sandals (Luke 10:4). Upon entering a house, they salute it with the greeting of "peace" and thus pronounce upon those who receive them the salvation that attends God's eschatological rule (Luke 10:5-6). Should they be turned out, their greeting of peace returns to them, and the curse of eschatological judgment rests upon that house (Luke 10:6). Thus, through word and deed the disciples endeavor to awaken Israel to the imminent coming of the kingdom, pronouncing eschatological weal upon those who accept them (Luke 10:8-9) and eschatological woe upon upon those who turn them away (Luke 10:10-15).

If the ministry of the disciples stands under the sign of the eschatological harvest, it also stands under the sign of eschatological tribulation. The Roman emperor Hadrian reputedly once said of Israel that it was, in relation to the nations of the world, like a sheep among seventy wolves. In Q, this simile is employed to warn the disciples of the danger they face, not from the side of Gentiles, but from the side of Israel itself (Luke 10:3). Contemporary Israel is an "evil generation" (Luke 11:29). As its forefathers killed and persecuted the prophets (Luke 6:23; 11:49-51), so it has refused to repent at the preaching of John and of Jesus (Luke 7:33-34; 11:32). Because the disciples are not above their teacher, they, too, can expect to encounter persecution (Luke 6:22–23). They will be hauled before local Jewish authorities as disturbers of the peace (Luke 12:11–12), and in the courts they will be slandered and declared to be godless and impious people (Luke 6:22). And even as Jesus does not escape martyrdom in Israel, so the disciples, too, must be prepared to bear their cross (Luke 14:27) and to lose their life (Luke 17:33) as they discharge the ministry entrusted them.

SOTERIOLOGY

In this final section, our aim is to probe the concept of salvation found in Q. In conjunction with this, we shall also take a brief look at the community in which Q arose.

The Community of Q

Q gives the impression that it was written for a community of Christians which regarded itself as being in close touch with the ministry of the earthly Jesus himself. The members of this community appear to consider the disciples in Q to be representative of themselves. Hence, they see themselves as having been commissioned, like the disciples, to continue in Israel the earthly ministry of Jesus (Luke 10:1–3, 21–22).

The principal language of this community was no doubt Greek, as is evident from the circumstance that Q was written in Greek. Moreover, the constituency of the community was largely Jewish Christian in character. Although the community seems to be open to Gentiles, it does not seem to be conducting a "Gentile mission" per se. Thus, the parable of the great supper alludes in Q, not to two missions (Jewish and Gentile), but to Jesus' one mission to Israel, directed at more than one group (Luke 14:16–24).[22] The anomaly in Q is that passages that otherwise might be understood to point to a Gentile mission tend to be used to convey a negative evaluation of Israel. The pericope on the healing of the centurion's slave, for example, culminates in a saying in which Jesus states that in Israel he has "not found" faith like that of this centurion (Luke 7:9). In the passages in which reference is made to "Jonah," to the "queen of the South," and to the "men of Nineveh," the intention is to censure Israel for its unbelief and to threaten it with judgment (Luke 11:29–32). On the matter of the Gentile mission as such, the community of Q appears to conceive of it, in line with OT thought (cf., e.g., Isa. 2:1–4; 25:6–8; Mic. 4:1–3), as an event that will take place at the end of the age when God shall have manifested his glorious rule in the sight of all the world. At that time, the Gentiles "will come from east and west, and from north and south, and sit at table in the kingdom of God" (Luke 13:29).

The question as to where this Q community should be located can be answered only in broad terms. At the heart of Jesus' instructions to his disciples about their mission, the names of the cities of Chorazin, Bethsaida, and Capernaum stand out prominently (Luke 10:13–15). Since the community of Q identifies itself with the disciples and their mission, northern Galilee commends itself well as the general region in which this community was active.

Yet another mark of the community of Q is that it almost certainly operated within the pale of Judaism. As we have noted, this was a community that held to the law and the tradition of the elders, as they were interpreted by Jesus, to be sure. This community understood its task to be that of carrying forward in Israel the ministry of Jesus. These factors do not suggest that the community had, in any formal sense, broken with Judaism.

As to date, Q seems to reflect a community that was active around the middle of the first century A.D. If one assumes that Matthew and Luke took Q up into their Gospels, and if one also allows for the fact that Q does not appear to make reference to the Jewish War (Matt. 22:7 is Matthaean redaction), one arrives at the early 60s as the latest possible date for its origin. Perhaps, then, Q is best thought of as having taken shape in the decades of the 40s and 50s.

The Locus of Salvation

A remarkable feature of Q is that no direct mention is made of the cross of Jesus. The one time the word "cross" occurs is in a saying of Jesus which speaks of the cost of discipleship: "Whoever does not bear his own cross and come after me, cannot be my disciple" (Luke 14:27). What can be inferred about Jesus from this passage, however, is clear: the community of Q conceives of his death in terms of martyrdom. In its eyes, Jesus has suffered the fate

It could also be that the Matth. + Luke common felt this to be so central a theme that they affix their own crucial affirmations.

of John the Baptist and of all the prophets (Luke 11:47–51; 13:34).

In stark contrast to Mark's Gospel, therefore, the cross is not the locus of salvation in Q. Instead, within the context of the history of salvation the members of the Q community look to the final judgment as the locus of salvation (Luke 12:8–9, 40; 17:24, 30). In the imagery of Q, at the final judgment Jesus Son of man will grant (table) fellowship in the kingdom of God (Luke 13:29; 14:16, 24) to those who have been his "faithful slaves" (Luke 12:42–44), i.e., to those who have "heard and done" his words and have "acknowledged him before men" (Luke 6:47; 12:8). In similar fashion, he will consign to torment those who have not been faithful slaves (Luke 12:45–46) or who, like Israel, have refused to repent on hearing the message of the nearness of God's kingdom or on witnessing the powerful acts that portend its glorious appearance (Luke 10:13–15; 11:29–32; 12:45–46).

But if the future is the locus of salvation, the members of the Q community nevertheless view the present as standing under the influence of the future (Luke 6:20; 11:20). As these Christians see it, "now" is the time of the eschatological harvest (Luke 10:2). "Now" is the time the risen Jesus calls them to forsake home, family, and possessions to wander from place to place in Israel summoning people through word and mighty deed to repentance (Luke 10:3–16). Like the prophets, John, and Jesus, they, too, must suffer persecution (Luke 6:22–23; 12:4–5). Still, they endure it, for those who are brought to repentance through their ministry become, like them, disciples of Jesus and enter into the sphere of God's end-time rule (Luke 10:23–24). To those who enter this sphere, the risen Jesus reveals God as Father and gives insight into God's purposes (Luke 10:21–22; 11:2). He also reveals himself as the supreme agent of God and the coming Son of man (Luke 10:22). In response to such revelation, Jesus' disciples do God's will as he has interpreted it, and practice toward "brother" and enemy alike the ethic of radical love (Luke 6:27–36, 46–48).

Oriented toward the future, therefore, the community of Q discharges its mission in Israel. Final salvation for this community attends the transcendent Son of man. Hence, it awaits with eager anticipation his sudden revelation from heaven as the Judge of all (Luke 12:8–9, 40; 17:24, 30).

NOTES

1. For a survey of some of the more recent trends in the study of Q, see: R. D. Worden, "Redaction Criticism of Q: A Survey," *Journal of Biblical Literature,* 94 (1975), 532–46.

2. A synopsis in Greek and German that contains only the supposed text of Q is that of S. Schulz, *Griechisch-deutsche Synopse der Q-Ueberlieferung* (Zürich: Theologischer Verlag, 1972). The best reconstruction of the Greek text of Q to date, however, is that of A. Polag, *Fragmenta Q* (Neukirchen-Vluyn: Neukirchener Verlag, 1979). For a concordance to Q, cf. R. A. Edwards, *A Concordance to Q* (Sources for Biblical Study 7; Missoula, Mont.: Scholars, 1975).

3. Cf., e.g., W. G. Kümmel, *Introduction to the New Testament,* tr. H. C. Kee (revised ed.; Nashville: Abingdon, 1975), p. 63.

4. On the origin of the sign "Q," cf. L. H. Silbermann ("Whence *Siglum* Q? A Conjecture," *Journal of Biblical Literature,* 98 [1979], 287–88), who concludes that the young German scholars of the 1890s, J. Weiss, P. Wernle, and W. Bousset, appropriated this sign from the OT scholar J. Wellhausen.

5. Cf. R. A. Edwards, *A Theology of Q* (Philadelphia: Fortress, 1976).

6. For a list of the names of scholars who hold that the Q materials available to Matthew and Luke were oral in nature, cf. Kümmel, *Introduction to the New Testament,* p. 64 n. 54.

7. Cf., e.g., Luke 3:7–9, 16–17 // Matt. 3:7–12; Luke 4:3–13 // Matt. 4:3–11; Luke 7:22–23 // Matt. 11:4–6; Luke 11:24–26 // Matt. 12:43–45; Luke 12:42–46 // Matt. 24:45–51.

8. Cf. C. E. Carlston and D. Norlin, "Once More Statistics and Q," *Harvard Theological Review,* 64 (1971), 68, 70–72.

9. Cf. V. Taylor, "The Original Order of Q," *New Testament Essays* (London: Epworth, 1970), pp. 95–118.

10. Cf. T. W. Manson, *The Sayings of Jesus* (reprint ed.; London: SCM, 1961), p. 16. Also B. H. Streeter, *The Four Gospels* (reprint ed.; London: Macmillan, 1956), p. 291.

11. Cf. A. M. Honoré, "A Statistical Study of the Synoptic Problem," *Novum Testamentum,* 10 (1968), 135.

12. Cf., e.g., S. Schulz, *Q: Spruchquelle der Evangelisten* (Zürich: Theologischer Verlag, 1972), pp. 40–44, 47–53, 165–75, 481–87; A. Polag, *Die Christologie der Logienquelle* (WMANT 45; Neukirchen-Vluyn: Neukirchener Verlag, 1977), pp. 10–17.

13. Cf., e.g., B. C. Butler, *The Originality of St. Matthew* (Cambridge: Cambridge University, 1951); and A. M. Farrer, "On Dispensing with Q," *Studies in the Gospels,* ed. D. E. Nineham (*Festschrift* R. H. Lightfoot; Oxford: Basil Blackwell, 1957), pp. 55–88.

14. Cf. esp. W. R. Farmer, *The Synoptic Problem* (New York: Macmillan, 1964), chap. 6. Also D. L. Dungan, "Mark—The Abridgement of Matthew and Luke," *Jesus and Man's Hope,* ed. D. G. Buttrick (Pittsburgh: Pittsburgh Theological Seminary, 1970), I, 51–97.

15. See above, n. 2.

16. John 12:21 shows that "Bethsaida," which is technically located in Lower Gaulanitis, could be regarded as a "city of Galilee."

17. Cf. the following articles in *Trajectories through Early Christianity* (Philadelphia: Fortress, 1971): J. M. Robinson, "*LOGOI SOPHON:* On

the Gattung of Q," pp. 71–113; H. Koester, "One Jesus and Four Primitive Gospels," pp. 158–204.

18. For a discussion of this topic, cf. Manson, *The Sayings of Jesus,* pp. 94–106.

19. For an analysis of the term "this generation" in Q, cf. D. Lührmann, *Die Redaktion der Logienquelle* (WMANT 33; Neukirchen-Vluyn: Neukirchener Verlag, 1969), pp. 24–48.

20. Cf. G. Theissen, "Itinerant Radicalism: The Tradition of Jesus Sayings from the Perspective of the Sociology of Literature," *Radical Religion,* 2 (1975), 84–93; idem, *Sociology of Early Palestinian Christianity,* tr. J. Bowden (Philadelphia: Fortress, 1978).

21. On this topic of the ministry of the disciples in Q, cf. also P. Hoffmann, *Studien zur Theologie der Logienquelle* (NTAbh 8; Münster: Aschendorff, 1972), pp. 236–334.

22. Cf. Schulz, *Q: Die Spruchquelle der Evangelisten,* pp. 400–402.

CHAPTER TWO

MARK

Like the community of Q, the evangelist Mark looks to the end of all things and awaits the final coming of Jesus (13:24-27). The Jesus whom Mark awaits, however, is the Jesus who has above all died on the cross. In Mark's Gospel, therefore, it is the cross, not the parousia, that gives shape to his thought. Correlatively, this shift in orientation results in a noticeably different view of Jesus and of salvation.

THE ACCOMPLISHMENT OF MARK

Mark is the first one to write a "Gospel." Scholars are still hard at work trying to determine to what extent Mark's document is susceptible to rhetorical analysis along ancient lines[1] or compares favorably to other types of ancient literature, such as the memoirs of great personages or their biographies.[2] By any measurement, however, Mark's accomplishment is remarkable.[3] What he inherited from the tradition was a large cross section of disparate materials. They consisted of sayings of Jesus of various types and of stories about him which circulated independently of one another in oral form in Christian communities. They also consisted of larger blocks of material. Examples of such blocks of material are the debates of 2:1—3:6, the parables of chap. 4, the miracle stories in 4:35—6:52, and the teaching found in 10:1-45.[4] A longer piece of tradition likewise lies at the basis of the little apocalypse (chap. 13) and perhaps of the passion account as well (chaps. 14—15).[5]

As the recipient of these disparate traditions, Mark gave them literary shape and interpreted them theologically. He has penned, in effect, what may be termed a "kerygmatic story."

Mark's Gospel as a Kerygmatic Story

Mark's Gospel is a "story" in the sense that it presents a narrative account of the earthly ministry of Jesus of Nazareth. It divides itself roughly into a prologue (1:1–13 [15]) and two main parts.[6] The first main part (1:14—8:26) depicts Jesus as discharging in Galilee a ministry of preaching, gathering disciples, teaching, healing, and exorcising demons. The second main part (8:27—16:8) portrays him as undertaking a journey to Jerusalem, where he suffers, dies, and is raised.

As Mark tells his story about Jesus of Nazareth, he also puts it in context. Indeed, this context is as broad as the entire sweep of God's history of salvation. Thus, Mark begins his story with a quotation from the OT which characterizes the ministry of John the Baptist as the "fulfillment" of prophecy (1:2–3). Similarly, when Jesus embarks upon his public ministry at the end of the prologue, Mark has him proclaim that "the time is fulfilled" (1:15). As Mark describes it, therefore, the appearance of John and of Jesus means that the age of OT prophecy has passed and the eschatological age of fulfillment has begun.

For Mark, however, the eschatological age of fulfillment is better construed as the age of the gospel. The age of the gospel, in turn, extends from the time of John until the end of time, when Jesus shall return in power and glory. It encompasses the successive ministries of John (1:1–8), of Jesus and the pre-Easter disciples (1:14–15; 3:13–16; 6:6b–7, 12–13), and of the post-Easter disciples, or church (13:10; 14:9). Still, what is decisive in this sequence is plainly the ministry of Jesus, for the ministry of John is preparatory to it (1:1–8), the ministry of the pre-Easter disciples is an extension of it (6:12–13, 30), and the ministry of the post-Easter church is founded upon it (14:9).

But why should Mark be concerned to situate his story of the earthly ministry of Jesus within a context of history that runs from the time of OT prophecy to the end of time? Because he is not only a storyteller but a theologian, and he wants to raise the claim that it is exactly the earthly ministry of Jesus that is pivotal to the whole of God's dealings with humankind. This is a point to which we shall return shortly.

Mark, then, tells the story of Jesus from his baptism to his resurrection. But what kind of a story is it? Clearly, it is not a historical biography or a chronicle, because it contains too many factual gaps to serve as a written documentary on the life of Jesus. Besides, the reason Mark tells his story has to do with the circumstance that, for him, Jesus is unlike other persons who have died and are gone. By virtue of his resurrection, Jesus is not dead but lives (16:6). Mark writes of him precisely because the earthly Jesus of his story is one with the risen Jesus whom his community encounters in its preaching and teaching. Hence, as Mark himself indicates, his story is of the nature of "gospel," or "proclamation" (cf. 1:1). It is, therefore, a "kerygmatic story."

The Focal Point of Mark's Gospel

A story such as Mark's is obviously not told without a purpose. To get at this purpose, however, one needs to know where the story culminates. Skillfully, Mark guides the reader to this place with a series of unmistakable clues.

These clues are the oft-recurring allusions and predictions Mark makes concerning the fate of Jesus. They appear almost from the outset of his narrative. As early as the prologue, for example, Mark reports that Jesus does not begin his public ministry until after "John was handed over" into the custody of the authorities (1:14). Since John is the forerunner of Jesus, his fate is a sign already of what Jesus' fate will be (cf. 14:43–46).

The second such allusion occurs almost immediately. The first time Mark pictures Jesus as teaching, he calls attention to the distance that exists between Jesus and the Jewish leaders when he writes, ". . . for he was teaching them as one who had authority, and not as the scribes" (1:22).

Shortly after this scene Mark has the leaders of the Jews engage Jesus in a series of debates. In the course of these debates, Jesus makes a veiled reference to the fact that death lies before him: ". . . the days will come when the bridegroom is taken away from them [the disciples], and then they will fast in that day" (2:20). Indeed, Mark closes this entire cycle of debates on the ominous note that "the Pharisees . . . held counsel against him, how to destroy him" (3:6).

In close proximity to the latter passage is the pericope on the choosing of the twelve (3:13–19). As Mark cites Judas's name, he mentions specially that this is the one "who also betrayed him" (3:19). Next, Mark turns to the family of Jesus, and portrays him as coming into conflict with them (3:20-21, 31-35). This conflict, in turn, presages Jesus' later repudiation in the synagogue at Nazareth, where family, relatives, and villagers alike take offense at him (6: 1–5).

Nor does the Marcan Jesus fare any better with the Jewish people. In chap. 4, Jesus announces to his disciples, with an eye to the Jewish crowd (4:1–2), that the latter are "those outside" who are blind, deaf, and without understanding and to whom God does not impart the mystery of his kingdom (4:11–12).

On balance, then, one can see that Mark so develops his story that before he has narrated even six chapters he has pictured Jesus as being alienated from Israel. The upshot is that the only ones who still hold to him are his disciples. But with this state of affairs, Mark has also set the stage for the second half of his story (8:27—16:8). Here it is Jesus' three chief predictions that "the Son of man must suffer many things . . . and be killed" (8:31; 9:31; 10:33-34) and the statement that the "chief priests and the scribes . . . sought a way to destroy him" (11:18; cf. 3:6 and 12:12) which control the flow of the story. Add to these the fateful sayings of Jesus that Judas will betray him (14:18–21), Peter will deny him (14:30), and all the disciples will be offended at him (14:27), and the point has been reached where Mark has only to narrate the final segment of his story: his account of the suffering of Jesus which culminates in his death on the cross (15:25-41).

Accordingly, it is the scene of the crucifixion of Jesus which constitutes the appointed climax toward which the whole of Mark's story tends. Indeed, even the pericope of the empty tomb (16:1–8) attests to this. As the young man in white announces that "he [Jesus] has been raised, he is not here," it is significant that he refers to Jesus as "the one from Nazareth" who, even as the risen one, remains the crucified one (cf. Mark's use of the perfect tense in 16:6).

The insight that the crucifixion, in conjunction with the resurrection, constitutes the climax of Mark's story enables us to make two additional observations. The one observation has to do with the theological claim that Mark is advancing on behalf of Jesus. We stated above that Mark locates the earthly ministry of Jesus within the context of the whole of God's history of salvation. Mark does this, we said, to show that the earthly ministry of Jesus is pivotal to all of God's dealings with humankind. We have subsequently seen, however, that Mark so shapes his story that the earthly ministry of Jesus culminates in the cross. What this indicates, therefore, is that while Mark does indeed affirm that the earthly ministry of Jesus is pivotal to all of God's dealings with humankind, he attributes particular importance to the cross. For Mark it is the cross that is the decisive event in the history of salvation.

The second observation is that, if the crucifixion is the climax of Mark's story, we can expect that it will be the point at which several of the narrative lines running through this story will converge. That this is in fact the case we shall soon see. By way of anticipation, however, we can already say that there are at least three such lines that converge at the scene of the crucifixion. These concern (a) the overall movement of Mark's story as this reveals itself in the major summary passages Mark composes, (b) the secret of Jesus' identity as the royal Son of God, and (c) the inability of the disciples prior to Jesus' death and resurrection either to penetrate this secret or to comprehend his mission. Hence, should the question now be posed as to what the overall accomplishment of Mark is, the answer is this: Mark writes a kerygmatic story, which reaches its culmination in the crucifixion (and resurrection), in order to proclaim thereby that it is only in the light of the cross that one can truly perceive who Jesus is, what it means to be his disciple, and what God has effected in him for the salvation of humankind.

THE FIGURE OF JESUS[7]

The prologue of Mark's Gospel (1:1–13 [15]) does double duty: at one level, it serves as the beginning of the kerygmatic story Mark narrates; at another level, it informs the reader, as distinct from the characters in the story, as to who Jesus is. So as to place Jesus in the proper perspective, Mark tells first of John the Baptist (1:2–8).

John the Baptist in Mark's view is the forerunner of Jesus (1:2, 7). As he discharges his ministry at the Jordan river, he proclaims to those who come out to him: "After me comes one who is mightier than I, the thong of whose sandals I am not worthy to stoop down and untie" (1:7). In thus pointing away from himself toward the coming of the Mightier One, John sets the stage for the appearance of Jesus.

Jesus as the Messiah, the Son of God

John's prediction of the coming of the Mightier One is fulfilled at once in the arrival of Jesus from Galilee (1:9–13). Jesus is this Mightier One, for following his baptism by John, Jesus is described as seeing the heavens split apart and the Spirit descend upon him (1:10). In other words, Jesus is the Mightier One because he is one whom God uniquely empowers with his Holy Spirit.[8]

The descent of the Spirit upon Jesus is coupled with the declaration of a voice from heaven: "You are my beloved Son, with you I am well pleased" (1:11). These words are from Gen. 22:2, Ps. 2:7, and Isa. 42:1. They characterize Jesus as the only, or unique, Son whom God has chosen for eschatological ministry in Israel. A glance at Ps. 2:7 lends further substance to the key predication "my Son." Here it is the king-designate of Judah, standing in the line of David, who on his day of coronation is called God's "anointed" ("Christ," or "Messiah") and God's "son" (Ps. 2:2, 6–7). Who, then, is this Jesus, the Mightier One, whom God at his baptism empowers with his Holy Spirit for eschatological ministry? He is the long-awaited Davidic Messiah, the royal Son of God, exactly as Mark also writes in the superscription of his Gospel: "The beginning of the gospel of Jesus Messiah, the Son of God" (1:1).

Mark shows in the opening scenes of Jesus' public ministry precisely what it means for him to present Jesus as the royal Son of God whom God has empowered for messianic activity. With divine authority (*exousia*), Jesus Son of God proclaims to Israel the nearness of the kingdom of God (1:14–15), calls his initial disciples (1:16–20), teaches "not as the scribes" (1:22), and heals the sick and exorcises demons, thus "plundering" Satan's domain (1:32–34; 3:22–27).

But by the same token, from the outset of Jesus' ministry Mark likewise shrouds his identity as the Son of God in a veil of secrecy. If God and such supernatural beings as the demons know of the divine sonship of Jesus (1:11, 24, 34; 3:11–12), the human characters who interact with him do not. In point of fact, Mark so guides the development of his story that only in stages does he permit the various aspects of Jesus' identity to come to light. Questions are raised as to who Jesus is, answers are given that are either false, only partially correct, or correct but not rightly perceived, but not until the end of his story, not until Jesus' death and resurrection, does Mark fully lift the veil that otherwise conceals the mystery of Jesus' person. Why does Mark proceed in this fashion? Because he wants to show that the identity of Jesus as the royal Son of God is inextricably bound up with his destiny, i.e., with his obedient willingness to go the way of the cross (cf. 14:35-36).

To begin with, then, it is solely such transcendent beings as God and the demons who know that Jesus is the royal Son of God (1:11, 24, 34; 3:11). Nevertheless, their knowledge remains hidden from the human characters in Mark's story. When God, for instance, declares Jesus at his baptism to be "my Son," it is Jesus alone to whom these words are spoken (1:11). When the demons shout aloud that Jesus is the Son of God, Jesus suppresses their cries of recognition (cf. esp. 1:34; 3:11-12).

Although it is not until the very end of his story that some of the human characters become privy to the knowledge that Jesus is the Son of God, Mark arranges from the beginning for representative persons to raise the question as to who Jesus is. It is with an eye to Jesus, for example, that the amazed people in the synagogue at Capernaum, having witnessed the exorcism of an unclean spirit, ask, "What is this? A new teaching with authority!" (1:27). Similarly, after Jesus has stilled the storm on the sea, the disciples are left wondering, "Who, then, is this, that even wind and sea obey him?" (4:41). And in the synagogue at Nazareth, where Jesus is rejected, the townspeople query one another, "Is not this the carpenter, the son of Mary . . . ?" (6:3).

On the heels of these questions, Mark provides answers in his story as to who people think that Jesus is. Some, like king Herod, believe that he is John the Baptist raised from the dead (6:14, 16). Others suppose that he is Elijah (6:15). And still others consider him to be a prophet, perhaps one of the great prophets of old (6:15).

These answers, however, are all false. Mark indicates this by contrasting them with an estimate of Jesus which is, on the one hand, correct but, on the other hand, only partially so. Thus, Jesus asks his disciples in the environs of Caesarea Philippi who people say that he is (8:27). Their reply repeats the answers cited above (8:28). In response to this, Jesus poses a counterquestion, "And you, who do you say that I am?" (8:29). At this, Peter affirms, "You are the Messiah!" (8:29).

The reason Peter's affirmation is correct, but only partially so, is that the designation "Messiah," as Mark has revealed in his prologue, cannot stand by itself but must be further interpreted in terms of the title Son of God (cf. 1:1 to 1:10–11). Indeed, to supplement Peter's confession Mark presents the story of the transfiguration (9: 2–8). Here before Peter, James, and John, Mark portrays Jesus as being transfigured and the voice from the cloud as announcing, "This is my beloved Son, hear him!" (9:3, 7). These words, of course, are a reiteration for the most part of the words spoken at the baptism (1:11). The important new development, however, is that if there they were addressed to Jesus alone, here they are addressed to the disciples. Still, despite this announcement Mark makes it plain that the secret of Jesus' divine sonship remains intact. This is the case because the disciples will not comprehend what it is they have seen and heard until after the crucifixion and resurrection (9:5–6, 9–10; 14:28; 16:7).

The next stage in the progressive unveiling of Jesus' identity occurs in the pericope of the healing of blind Bartimaeus (10:46–52). The blind beggar, undeterred by the opposition of many in the crowd, appeals to Jesus as the Son of David to have mercy on him (10:47–48). Acceding to Bartimaeus's appeal, Jesus has him summoned and grants his request for the gift of his sight (10:49–52). Hence, Mark, in depicting Jesus as healing one who cries out to him in faith as the Son of David (10:52), attests to the basic correctness of this title.

Not only this, but Mark also places the entry of Jesus into Jerusalem under the aegis of this title (11:1–11). This is evident from the numerous messianic allusions associated with David which Mark here applies to Jesus. Thus, the entire pericope is informed by such messianically interpreted passages as Zech. 9:9 and Gen. 49:11.[9] In sending his disciples to bring the colt on which he will ride (11:1–7), Jesus makes use of the royal prerogative by which a king can requisition an animal for his use (cf. 1 Sam. 8:10–11, 17).[10] The "colt" on which Jesus sits (11:2–7) is the symbol par excellence for the messianic mount. The spreading of garments and of leafy branches on the road (11:8) are gestures of adoration that

befit a king (cf. 2 Kings 9:13). And in the antiphonal acclamation
of those who accompany Jesus, he is hailed with shouts to God that
assume the form of a petition for salvation ("Hosanna" [cf. Ps.
118:25]) and is praised as the one who comes on the authority of
God and can therefore be expected to establish "the Kingdom of our
father David" (11:9–10). In Mark's eyes, therefore, Jesus is in
truth the Son of David.

But as with "Messiah," "Son of David," too, is only a partially
correct designation for Jesus. Mark reveals this in the pericope on
the question about David's Son (12:35–37). The issue Jesus raises
while teaching in the temple has to do with the "sonship" of the
Messiah (12:35, 37). If in scripture King David of old calls the
Messiah "Lord," i.e., acknowledges that the Messiah is of higher
station and authority than he, how can the Messiah be regarded
merely as the Son of David?

It is necessary to observe that Jesus does not pose this question
within the framework of a debate. Debate with Jesus ended at 12:34,
and this pericope follows. Consequently, Mark is not putting Jesus
in the position of striking down a false opinion. Moreover, neither
does Jesus deny that the Messiah is the Son of David. Instead, his
contention is that the Messiah, whom the scribes, too, think of as
being the Son of David, must at the same time be held to be of yet
higher station. Who must the Messiah be if he is to be at once
Davidic and yet of higher station than David? As the reader knows
from the baptism and the transfiguration, he is the Son of God.[11]

The pericope on the trial of Jesus before the Sanhedrin (14:53–
65) marks the penultimate stage in the gradual disclosure of the
secret of Jesus' identity. The high priest puts the question to Jesus,
"Are you the Messiah, the Son of the Blessed (God)?" (14:61).
To this question Jesus firmly replies, "I am!" (14:62). With this
unambiguous answer, Mark's story has ostensibly reached the dra-
matic climax where the secret of Jesus' divine sonship has been
revealed. Yet, because the high priest and the Sanhedrin construe
Jesus' reply as "blasphemy" (14:64), they can be seen, ironically,
not to have penetrated the secret. Hence, it continues unbroken.

It is in Mark's narration of Jesus' crucifixion and resurrection
that the secret of his divine sonship finally surfaces. The chief
passages are 15:39 and 16:6, which are anticipated in 12:1–12 by

the parable of the wicked husbandmen. Toward the end of this parable, Mark employs the "stone(s)—son(s)" imagery of the OT[12] in order to allude to the death—resurrection and the resurrection—vindication of Jesus: "The stone which the builders rejected, this has become the head of the corner" (12:10). As for the parable itself, Mark draws on the familiar language of the baptism and the transfiguration to indicate that the "stone—son" to whom he is alluding is Jesus Son of God: the "beloved son" (12:6), whom the lord of the vineyard designates as "my son" (12:6), is the one who is killed by the tenants but vindicated by his father (12:8–9).

The parable of the wicked husbandmen points ahead to the narrative of the passion and resurrection. Here for the first time Mark permits one of the human characters in his story to declare, unencumbered by any restrictions whatever, that Jesus is the Son of God. The Roman centurion, as he stands opposite Jesus and witnesses his death on the cross, confesses aloud, "Truly this man was the Son of God!" (15:39). Accordingly, the cross is the place within Mark's story where the secret of Jesus' divine sonship comes to full disclosure.

But even as the resurrected one, Mark's Jesus does not cease to be the "crucified one." In the pericope on the empty tomb (16:1–8), for instance, the young man in white refers to the risen Jesus as the one who, having been crucified, remains the crucified one (16:6; cf. *estaurōmenon* in the perfect tense). And who precisely is this "crucified" Jesus who has been raised by God? He is Jesus in his status as the royal Son of God. This is apparent for three reasons. First, because the use of the term the "crucified one" in 16:6 calls to mind the scene of the crucifixion, which culminates in the centurion's confession of Jesus as the Son of God (15:39). Second, because the resurrection of the crucified one is the event in which the prophecy appended to the parable of the wicked husbandmen comes to fulfillment: it is in raising Jesus from the dead that God places the "rejected stone," i.e., his Son, "at the head of the corner" (12:6, 8, 10–11). And third, because the passage 13:32 indicates that also in the time between the resurrection and the parousia, Mark conceives of Jesus as the Son of God.

It is, therefore, the crucified and resurrected Son of God about whom the young man in white is speaking when he predicts that the disciples will "see" him in Galilee (16:6–7; cf. 14:28). Since Mark has consistently shown that the prophecies of scripture (1:2–3; 9:12–13; 14:49), of John the Baptist (1:7–8), and of Jesus (8:31; 9:31; 10:33–34) are trustworthy and come to pass, the reader can rest assured that this prediction, too, has not failed of fulfillment.[13] What this means for the disciples, however, is that they, too, in "seeing" Jesus as the crucified and resurrected Son of God, are enabled to perceive the secret of his identity. Hence, Mark's intimation is that at the projected meeting in Galilee, the disciples at last "see" what previously they had been unable to "see" (cf. 9:1–10).

With the crucifixion and resurrection, then, Mark discloses the secret of Jesus' divine sonship. This secret is, as we mentioned earlier, one of the three main narrative lines that can be traced throughout Mark's story. Its purpose is to lead the reader to assume a position in the time beyond the cross and resurrection and to recognize that, without a true perception of Jesus' destiny, one cannot arrive at a true perception of his identity as the royal Son of God. To put it another way, the purpose of the secret is to bring the reader to the realization that to confess Jesus to be the Son of God is to confess him, even as the risen one, to be the one appointed by God not only to preach, call disciples, teach, heal, and exorcise demons, but also, and especially, to die upon the cross (15:39; 16:6).

Jesus as the Son of Man

This survey of Jesus as the royal Messiah, the Son of God, still leaves us with a problem. What is one to make of Mark's use of the title Son of man?

To get at this, it is crucial to observe how Mark relates "Son of man" to the other titles he employs. It appears that he does not include it within the circle of such titles as "Messiah," "King," "Son of David," and "Son of God." Three factors support this view. For one thing, Mark places the latter titles in apposition to one another ("Jesus Messiah, the Son of God" [1:1]; "the Messiah, the Son of the Blessed" [14:61]; "the Messiah, the King of Israel" [15:32]; cf. 12:35: "the Messiah is the Son of David"); but he never places "Messiah" and "Son of man" in apposition to each other. For another thing, while Jesus is addressed in faith as the "Son of David"

(10:47–49, 52) and in ironic mockery as "King" (15:18, 32), and while he is confessed to be the "Messiah" (8:29) and the "Son of God" (15:39), never is he ever confessed to be the Son of man or even addressed as such. And last, despite the fact that Jesus openly refers to himself in the presence of both the scribes (2:6, 10) and the Pharisees (2:24, 28) as the Son of man, so that this is no secret to his enemies, the high priest does not ask him at his trial before the Sanhedrin whether he is the Messiah, the Son of man, but whether he is the Messiah, the Son of the Blessed (God) (14:61).

Standing apart as it does from what we may term the "messianic" titles of Mark's Gospel, the title Son of man functions differently from them. To begin with, there is no aura of secrecy surrounding it like that which surrounds the title Son of God. Jesus calls himself the Son of man in the full hearing of the scribes and the Pharisees (2:6, 10, 24, 28).

In the second place, indicative of the title Son of man is a strong note of opposition. At 2:10 and 2:28, Jesus designates himself as the Son of man in scenes in which his enemies take offense at the authority with which he acts. In the passion predictions and related passages, Jesus again designates himself as the Son of man as he teaches his disciples what his enemies are soon to do to him: Judas will betray him (9:31; 10:33; 14:21, 41); and he will suffer at the hands of the Jewish leaders and Gentiles and be killed (8:31; 9:12, 31; 10:33–34). At 10:42–45, Jesus likewise designates himself as the Son of man as he holds himself up to his disciples, in conscious opposition to the ways of the world, as the model of self-sacrificial service they are to emulate in their own lives in the world. And in the parousia passages, Jesus once more designates himself as the Son of man as he prophesies his vindication before the world: he, the Son of man, who has been made to suffer at the hands of Jew and Gentile, will come at the end of time in great power and glory as Judge and inaugurate in the sight of all the world God's consum-. mated kingdom (8:38; 9:1; 13:24–27).

It is also in the light of the preceding that the parousia passage 14:62 is to be understood. In 14:61, the high priest asks Jesus whether he is "the Messiah, the Son of the Blessed (God)." Jesus replies in the affirmative, "I am!" (14:62). Then he goes on to say, ". . . and you will see the Son of man sitting on the right hand of power and coming with the clouds of heaven" (14:62). The sense of Jesus' words is this: Inasmuch as you have asked me whether I am the Son of God in order to condemn me, it will be as your Judge that you will see the Son of man coming in glory at the latter day (cf. 8:38).

Accordingly, Mark's use of the title Son of man contrasts sharply with his use of the "messianic" titles. This contrast can be described in three sets of antithetic statements. (a) The major focus of the messianic titles is on a true perception as to who Jesus is. The major focus of the title Son of man is on Jesus as he interacts with his enemies and predicts the suffering he must endure at their hands and his future vindication at the end of time. (b) The messianic titles move on a trajectory that aims at the centurion's confession at the crucifixion that Jesus is the Son of God (15:39) and the prediction that the disciples will "see" him in Galilee as this crucified one whom God has raised from the dead (16:6–7). The title Son of man moves on a trajectory that aims at the second coming of Jesus when all people, and thus both his enemies and his disciples, will "see" him as Savior or Judge (8:38; 9:1; 13:24–27; 14:62). (c) In sum, the mark of the messianic titles is that Jesus should be confessed to be the royal Son of God whose divinely wrought destiny is the cross. The mark of the title Son of man is that Jesus should stand forth in the suffering he predicts for himself as the example his disciples are to follow as they make their way in the world and the one whose final coming, or vindication, they can await in confidence as their vindication as well.

Does this broad schema mean, then, that the messianic titles on the one hand and the title Son of man on the other have nothing, finally, to bind them together? Not at all! For in 8:38 Mark speaks of the Son of man as coming in the glory "of his Father." As this phrase shows, Jesus, the *royal Son of man* who carries out the end-time judgment, remains, to Mark's way of thinking, the *royal Son of God* (cf. also 13:32).

THE MISSION OF JESUS

Mark's story of the ministry of Jesus does not begin with Jesus himself but with John the Baptist (1:1–8). John is a "prophet" (11:32), and his garment of camel-hair, his leather belt, and his food of locusts and wild honey attest to this (1:6; cf. 2 Kings 1:8; Zech. 13:4). At the same time, John is a prophet like none other, for he is God's eschatological "messenger" (1:2), the "voice" that "cries in the desert" (1:3), Elijah redivivus (9:13).

John's task in the history of salvation is to "prepare the way" for Jesus Messiah, the Son of God (1:1, 2–3). At God's appointed time, he makes his appearance in the desert of the lower Jordan valley (1:4). He proclaims repentance, i.e., the turning from evil toward God (1:4), and baptizes those who confess their sins (1:5). If in Q his preaching is laden with stern pronouncements of judgment, the same is not true in Mark's portrait of him. All the country of Judea and all the people of Jerusalem go out to John to be baptized (1:5). In this way, he "restores all things," even as it was expected of Elijah (9:2–13; Mal. 4:5). Thus, he fulfills his God-given purpose and readies all Israel for the coming of its Messiah (1:7–8).

Following in the wake of John, Jesus embarks in Mark's Gospel on his public ministry. It is oriented geographically to Galilee and Jerusalem: after widespread activity in Galilee (1:14—8:26), Jesus undertakes a journey to Jerusalem (8:27—10:52), where he suffers, dies, and is raised (11:1—16:8). The object of Jesus' ministry, therefore, is specifically Israel,[14] although this by no means precludes his ministering to Gentiles as well.[15] During his stay in Galilee,[16] Jesus is "at home," if anywhere, in Capernaum.[17]

By and large, however, the picture Mark paints of Jesus is that of an itinerant teacher and healer who is continually on the move. He goes in and out of Capernaum (cf. 1:21 and 1:35; 2:1 and 2:13; 9:33 and 10:1). He makes his way to the sea (1:16; 2:13; 3:7; 4:1; 5:21). He wanders among the villages[18] and cities (6:56) of Galilee. Sometimes he searches out deserted places for prayer or rest (1:35, 45; 6:31). Included in his journeys are trips across the sea and back (4:35; 5:1, 21; 6:45; 8:13). Conversely, news of Jesus is spread abroad, not only throughout the regions of Galilee but even beyond (1:28, 45; 3:8; 6:14, 54–56). The result is that people from Galilee, Judea, Jerusalem, Idumea, Perea, and about Tyre and Sidon stream to him (3:7–8). It is in the sight of large crowds that Jesus discharges his ministry.[19]

The movement of Jesus in Israel, which seems to be somewhat

"helter-skelter" in the first half of the Gospel, is given cohesion and direction by two sets of three summary passages. The first set of three appears in the first main part of the Gospel (1:32–39; 3:7–12; 6:53–56). The second set of three appears in the second main part (8:31; 9:31; 10:33–34). Taken together, they reveal that the focus of Jesus' wanderings in Galilee is his ministry of word and deed (1:14–8:26), whereas the focus of his journey to Jerusalem and stay there is his suffering, death, and rising (8:27—16:8). If, as we have seen, the secret of Jesus' divine sonship constitutes the first of three major narrative lines that run like red threads through Mark's story, these summary passages constitute the second such narrative line.

Before we turn to Jesus' ministry of preaching, one other matter begs for consideration. Foundational to the whole of Jesus' public ministry is his baptism and temptation. At his baptism, Jesus is, we recall, empowered with the Holy Spirit and declared by God to be his Son (1:9–11). So equipped with the Spirit, Jesus Son of God withstands the temptation of Satan for forty days in the desert, thereby "binding," or subduing, him (1:12–13; cf. 3:27). Hence, as Jesus Messiah, the Son of God, takes up his eschatological ministry of preaching, calling disciples, teaching, healing, exorcising demons, and suffering and dying, he is to be seen as the supreme agent of God who acts on the divine authority of God.

Jesus' Ministry of Preaching

Jesus does not begin his public ministry in Mark's story until after John the Baptist has been arrested (1:14). His initial act is to "preach" (1:14),[20] and he traverses the whole of Galilee (1:38–39) as he announces in the synagogues of Israel: "The time is fulfilled and the kingdom of God is at hand; repent, and believe in the gospel" (1:14–15). This summary contains four elements that Mark regards as basic to the preaching of Jesus: reference to the "fullness of time," the "kingdom of God," "repentance and faith," and the "gospel." The concept of the "fullness of time" we have already discussed: it has to do with Mark's view of the history of salvation, according to which the age of OT prophecy has passed and the eschatological age of the gospel has dawned. We turn our attention, therefore, to the other three elements of the summary.

Mark writes of Jesus that he both proclaims the gospel and summons people to believe in the gospel (1:14–15). The gospel Jesus proclaims is characterized by Mark as the "gospel of God" (1:14). Still, Mark shows in 14:9 that Jesus himself also belongs to the gospel. Hence, in Mark's scheme of things "the gospel" has a christological center (cf. 1:1). How, then, does Mark understand the expression the "gospel of God"? Summarily stated, it is the good news that God, with his eschatological rule, is at work in Jesus Messiah, his Son—in his ministry and passion and resurrection and in the future proclamation of these—to effect repentance and faith and consequently salvation.

Mention was just made of God's eschatological rule. The term the "rule of God" is, as we know, simply a paraphrase of the term the "kingdom of God." The topic of the kingdom, in turn, is the controlling element in Jesus' preaching (1:15). How does Mark conceive of it?

Jesus' announcement is that the "kingdom of God is at hand" (1:14). Thus, like the community of Q Mark holds to the imminent expectation of the end. "There are some standing here," asserts Jesus, "who will not taste of death before they see the kingdom of God come with power" (9:1). Of Joseph of Arimathea Mark says: he is one who is "also himself looking for the kingdom of God" (15:43). And concerning himself the Marcan Jesus vows: "Truly I say to you, I shall not drink of the fruit of the vine until that day when I drink it new in the kingdom of God" (14:25).

As Mark sees it, therefore, in the near future Jesus Son of man will come on the clouds of heaven with great power and glory to usher in the consummated kingdom of God (9:1; 13:24–27). When he comes, he will carry out the final judgment (8:38; 13:24–27). Hanging in the balance will be salvation or condemnation for all (8:38—9:1; 13:26-27; 14:62). People will either "enter into the kingdom," i.e., into "life,"[21] or they will be "cast into Gehenna" (9:43, 45, 47).

But the kingdom of God, as Mark describes it, is not only a future reality. It is a present reality as well. Children, for example, can be said to "receive" it (10:14–15), or a scribe to be "not far" from it (12:34). As a present reality, the kingdom is also hidden. It is hidden in Jesus and in the gospel. Israel encounters the kingdom in the earthly Jesus, in his gospel message and in his deeds (1:14–15); the Gentiles encounter the kingdom in the world-wide proclamation of the gospel about Jesus (13:10; 14:9).

Because the kingdom is a present reality, a close correlation exists in Mark's thought between it and the secret of the divine sonship of Jesus. As Israel confronts Jesus, it does not comprehend that he is its royal Messiah, the Son of God. By the same token, neither does it comprehend that in him God is present with his end-time rule. In point of fact, to understand the one would be to understand the other. Then, too, for the very reason that Israel is blind to the presence of the kingdom in Jesus, Jesus declares with an eye to the Jews that the "mystery of the Kingdom of God" has not been given to them and that they are without perception and understanding (4:1–2, 11–12).

There is one place in his Gospel where Mark directly relates the kingdom as a present reality to the kingdom as a future reality. Through the medium of the parables of the seed growing secretly (4:26–29) and of the mustard seed (4:30–32), Mark shows how the one sets in motion a "process of growth," or sequence of events, that necessarily issues in the other: from tiny, even hidden, beginnings in the ministry and passion and resurrection of Jesus Messiah, the Son of God, the kingdom moves inexorably toward its consummation at the end of history when Jesus Son of man will appear in splendor as the Judge of all. This is the fuller statement of what Mark means by "the secret of the kingdom of God" (4:11).

The final element in Jesus' proclamation to Israel is the summons, ". . . repent, and believe in the gospel" (1:15). "Repentance" and "faith" to Mark's mind are two sides of the same coin. Repentance connotes "radical conversion": an unconditional turning away from evil and all that is against God.[22] Faith connotes "radical confidence," an unconditional turning toward the gospel in complete trust. For Mark, however, to place one's trust in the gospel is to place one's trust in the one who stands at the center of the gospel, namely, Jesus (cf. 9:42 to 9:41; 8:35; 10:29). In preaching to Israel, therefore, Jesus is calling Israel to decision. Those who heed his summons will become his disciples (8:34), live in the sphere of God's end-time Rule (1:15; 4:26–32; 10:15), and at the latter day be saved (13:26–27). Those who refuse his summons will align themselves with "this adulterous and sinful generation" and at the latter day incur judgment (8:38).

We have treated at some length the various aspects of the preaching of Jesus as Mark summarizes it in the words, "The time is fulfilled and the kingdom of God is at hand; repent, and believe in the gospel" (1:14–15). Put briefly, this preaching announces that the end-time age has dawned and that God in the person of his Son has drawn near with his rule; in the face of this radically new situation, what one must do is to turn from evil and to place one's trust in this good news Jesus is announcing, which is to say that one is to place one's trust in Jesus himself.

Jesus' Ministry of Teaching

Of the various activities in which the Marcan Jesus engages in the course of his ministry in Israel, "teaching" is what is most typical of him. It is the thing he is "accustomed" to do (10:1). Moreover, it is as "teacher" and "rabbi" (or "rabboni," 10:51) that he is publicly known (14:14). These are equivalent terms of human respect by which all manner of people either address Jesus or refer to him: one of the disciples (13:1), all of the disciples (4:38), Peter (9:5; 11:21), John (9:38), James and John (10:35), Judas (14:45), the messengers sent to Jairus (5:35), a father with an epileptic son (9:17), a rich man (10:17, 20), blind Bartimaeus (10:51), Pharisees and Herodians (12:14), Sadducees (12:19), and a scribe (12:32).

In reality, of course, Jesus is far more in Mark's eyes than the eminent teacher the Israelite public of his story knows him to be (10:1; 12:14; 14:49). He is the Messiah, the royal Son of God (1:11). As God's Son, he is endowed with the Spirit; in him, God's end-time kingdom, or rule, is a present reality. When, therefore, Jesus "preaches," it is with authority, for his words are imbued with the power of the kingdom. By the same token, this is not one whit less true when Jesus "teaches."[23]

Thus, the first time Jesus teaches in the Gospel story, Mark remarks of him: "And they [the people in the synagogue at Capernaum] were astonished at his teaching, for he taught them as one who had authority" (1:22). Also, when Jesus expels an unclean spirit from a man by the word of his mouth, these same people exclaim: "What is this? A new teaching with authority!" (1:27). The point is, the power of the kingdom inheres in the teaching of Jesus; it is "new" and qualitatively different from any teaching ever before heard in Israel.

The major topics Jesus treats in his teaching in Mark's story are such as the following: the kingdom of God, the will of God, his own impending passion, matters pertaining to discipleship, and pressing issues having to do with the time before the end. Because we treat all of these topics save for the one about the will of God elsewhere, we shall concentrate on that here.

As teacher of the will of God, the Marcan Jesus stands forth as sovereign in his knowledge and pronouncements (cf. 3:35). By laying bare the intention of the law, he reveals what the will of God is. Asked by a scribe, "Which commandment is the first of all?" (12:28), Jesus recites the two "chief" commandments of Moses (12:28–34). These enjoin "love of God" (12:29–30; Deut. 6:4–5) and "love of neighbor" (12:31; Lev. 19:18). Hence, loving God and loving the neighbor are of the essence of what it means to do the will of God.

Unlike the Matthaean Jesus, the Marcan Jesus utters no antitheses in his teaching on the law (cf. Matt. 5:21–48). Instead, Jesus equates the word of Moses with the word of God (cf. 7:10 to 7:13; 12:26). In principle, therefore, the Marcan Jesus does not pit himself against Moses, but authoritatively interprets him (cf. 10:3–9; 12:19, 26–27).

This distinction, however, is a fine one, because there are two instances in which the Marcan Jesus plainly sets himself above Moses. On the question of defilement (7:14–23), Jesus' knowledge of the will of God leads him to pronounce all foods to be clean (7:15, 19). This pronouncement, in effect, abrogates the dietary laws of Moses (Lev. 11; Deut. 14). In similar fashion, Jesus also overrides Moses on the matter of divorce (10:1–12). As the Pharisees correctly observe, "Moses allows a man to write a certificate of divorce" (cf. Deut. 24:1, 3). To this Jesus rejoins that it is not God's will that divorce be allowed at all (10:5–12).

But if Jesus' knowledge of the will of God does not make him the opponent of Moses per se, it does embroil him in conflict with the leaders of Israel. Jesus clashes with the Pharisees over their interpretation of the law as it pertains to the sabbath (2:23–28; 3:1–6) or to paying taxes to Caesar (12:13–17). He disputes the contention of the Sadducees that the notion of the resurrection of the dead is without foundation in the law of Moses (12:18–27). He resists the attack that scribes and others make on his "style of life" as this relates to fasting (2:18–19) or to eating with tax-collectors and sinners (2:15–17). Indeed, he himself is critical of the scribes for their love of ostentation (12:38–39). And he also deplores the use to which the chief priests and the scribes have put the temple (11: 17–18).

In one other respect, Jesus' conflict with the leaders of Israel is also of note. Mark depicts Jesus as setting aside completely the Pharisaic "tradition of the elders" (7:1–13). With a view to this tradition, an oral supplement to the law of Moses which the Pharisees held to be as binding as the law itself, Jesus charges: "[You] make void the word of God through your tradition which you hand on" (7:13). On this issue, therefore, the Marcan Jesus assumes a strikingly different posture from the Jesus of Q.

Jesus' Ministry of Healing

Jesus' ministry of healing (1:34; 3:10) has to do with the "miracles," or "powerful acts," he performs. These powerful acts comprise roughly exorcisms, healings, and nature miracles. Significantly, Mark never designates them as "signs" or "wonders." On the contrary, it is the Pharisees who ask for a "sign" (8:11), and the false messiahs who perform "signs and wonders" (13:22). Proportionately, Mark recounts more miracle stories than any other evangelist. How does he deal with them?

Just as Jesus, the agent of God's kingdom, "preaches" and "teaches" with authority, so he also "acts" with authority.[24] The same power of the kingdom which inheres in the words of Jesus is likewise operative in his deeds. In the pericope on collusion with Satan (3:22–27), Mark explains how he understands the miraculous deeds of Jesus.

In this pericope, the scribes from Jerusalem charge Jesus with working in concert with Satan. They contend that it is by the prince of demons that he casts out demons (3:22). By way of rebuttal, Jesus demands to know: "How can Satan cast out Satan?" (3:23).

Then he declares: "If a kingdom is divided against itself, that kingdom will not be able to stand. . . . And if Satan has risen up against himself and is divided, he cannot stand, but is coming to an end!" (3:24, 26).

As this episode suggests, Mark views the exorcisms of Jesus as evidence of the cosmic clash between the kingdom of God and the kingdom of Satan. People who are ill, or in this case possessed by demons, are held to be in bondage to Satan. But in Jesus Messiah, his Son, God has drawn near with his end-time rule. Accordingly, as Jesus heals people of their afflictions, he is effectively "plundering" the kingdom of Satan (3:27). He is releasing these people from Satan's bondage and bringing them into the gracious sphere where they live under God's rule. He is, in short, "saving" them (6:56).

The three summary passages that guide the first half of Mark's story sketch a vivid picture of Jesus' ministry of healing (1:32–34; 3:7–12; 6:53–56). Through his powerful acts, Jesus becomes well-known in Capernaum (1:32–34), everywhere in Galilee (1:28), and even in the regions beyond (3:7–8). People throughout Palestine and from as far away as Tyre and Sidon flock to him (3:7–8). Indeed, so "well" does Jesus "do all things" that, even when he commands silence about a miracle he has performed, the news of it cannot be suppressed but must be proclaimed.[25]

Jesus' reputation as a healer and miracle-worker earns him a mixed response in Israel. There are some who are instinctively hostile toward him. His own family, for example, thinks of him as being "mad" (3:20–21). And the leaders of Israel accuse him of being possessed by Beelzebul, so that it is "by the prince of demons" that he "casts out demons" (3:22).

But family and enemies, Mark shows, have distorted opinions of Jesus. Indeed, the demons themselves know that he is in reality the Son of God (1:24, 34; 3:11). They recognize to their dread that God is present in him with his end-time rule to destroy both them (1:24, 27) and the whole of Satan's empire (3:23–27).

Next there are those individuals in Israel who hear of Jesus and find their way to him for help or healing. These individuals are depicted as persons of great faith (2:3, 5; 5:34, 36; 9:24; 10:46, 52). They trust that Jesus has the power to meet their needs. By exhibiting such trust in Jesus, they stand out, in effect, as "examples of faith."

Finally, there are the "many," or the "crowd." Their reaction to Jesus' powerful acts is that of astonishment and amazement (1:27; 2:12; 6:2; 7:37; cf. 5:42). Such amazement, however, does not impel them to confess Jesus to be the Messiah Son of God, the agent of the kingdom. This is because amazement is not an expression of faith, but suggests instead a lack of understanding (6:51–52). People who are amazed at Jesus can also take offense at him (6:2). Hence, the end of Jesus' ministry of healing in Israel, no less than that of his ministry of preaching and teaching, is the cross.

Jesus' Passion and Resurrection

The three summary passages that control the second half of Mark's story are the so-called passion predictions (8:31; 9:31; 10:33–34). Jesus utters them on his journey to Jerusalem (8:27—10:52) and tells of his suffering, death, and rising. These predictions document the failure of Jesus' ministry of preaching, teaching, and healing as far as Israel is concerned.

The leaders of Israel are Jesus' mortal enemies, and they take counsel to destroy him (11:18; cf. 3:6). In fact, they pick up where Satan left off (1:13) and endeavor to tempt him (8:11; 10:2; 12:15) and to entrap him in his speech (12:13). They look upon him as being a demoniac (3:30), and demand that he prove to them by means of a sign God should perform at his behest that his ministry has in truth been divinely authorized (8:11). With the help of Judas, who offers to betray him (14:10–11), they finally arrest him (14:43–46). They condemn him to death for blasphemy (14:53–65), secure the acquiescence of Pilate in carrying out their scheme (15:1–15), and see him brought by Roman soldiers to the cross (15:21–26). At the last, the Jewish people join them in calling for Jesus' crucifixion (15:8, 11–15). The question is: What theological significance does Mark associate with the cross and resurrection?

At his trial before the Sanhedrin, Jesus is condemned to death for affirming that he is indeed the Messiah, the Son of God (14:61–64). In the course of his trial, one of the charges lodged against him is that he was heard to say: "I will destroy this temple that is made with hands, and in three days I will build another, not made with hands" (14:58; cf. 2 Sam. 7:13–16).[26] As Mark develops his story, this claim, though advanced by false witnesses (14:57), nevertheless materializes. For at the death of Jesus, God causes the curtain of the temple to be torn in two (15:38). The curtain that is meant is in all probability the one that screened the holiest place. On the Day of Atonement each year, the high priest went behind it in order to make atonement for the sins of Israel. But if God, in tearing this curtain, signals the destruction of the temple, then he likewise signals the end of Israel's cult. For Mark, this theological truth necessarily follows, because through his death Jesus Messiah, the Son of God (15:32, 39), has made final atonement for sin. He has, in point of fact, brought to fulfillment the words he spoke at the passover meal he celebrated with his disciples: "This is my blood of the covenant, which is poured out for many" (14:24; cf. 10:45). Then, too, as the reference to "many" reveals, this covenant is intended not merely for Jews, but for Gentiles as well. What, therefore, does Jesus Messiah, the Son of God, accomplish in the cross? In Mark's story, he brings the cult of Israel to an end and makes atonement for sin "once for all."

But there is more to it than this. Jesus also "builds another temple" (14:58; cf. 2 Sam. 7:13–16). Upon the death of Jesus, the centurion confesses him to be the "Son of God" (15:39). In addition, the promise is given the disciples that, following the resurrection, they will see the "smitten shepherd," the "crucified one," in Galilee (14:27–28; 16:7). Consequently, Jesus builds another temple by founding, on the basis of his cross, a new community (cf. 10:29–30). This community will embrace people of both Jewish (the disciples) and Gentile (the Roman centurion) origins. It is, in Mark's theology, the eschatological community of the new covenant. In its midst, Jesus, vindicated by God through his resurrection (12:10–11), will dwell as the new community partakes in its own cultic celebration of his body and blood (14:22–24). With this mention of the new community, we turn now to the topic of discipleship.

DISCIPLESHIP

There are three narrative lines, we said, that stand out prominently in Mark's story. The one narrative line comprises the six summary passages that govern the flow of his story: the three passages that occur in the first half of the Gospel (1:32–39; 3:7–12; 6:53–56); and the three passion-predictions that occur in the second half of the Gospel (8:31; 9:31; 10:33–34). A second narrative line has to do with the secret that Jesus is the Son of God. The third narrative line, concerning the disciples of Jesus, we shall take up in this section.

As Mark narrates it, Jesus Messiah, the Son of God, exercises the same divine authority in calling disciples as in preaching, teaching, and healing. Empowered by the Spirit (1:10–11), Jesus sovereignly summons his initial followers (1:16–20). They obey his call at once, forsaking their way of life in order to come after him (1:18, 20). As his followers, they relate to him as "teacher,"[27] and they, as "disciples," are "learners." In Jesus, God's end-time rule is a present reality, and they, in being joined to him, enter into its sphere.

The pericope on the choosing of the twelve (3:13–19) is the place to begin in order to get at Mark's conception of what it means to be a disciple of Jesus.[28] Jesus is depicted as authoritatively calling to himself "those whom he wanted" (3:13). In so doing, he "creates" the twelve in a manner that is reminiscent of God's creating the people of Israel (cf. Isa. 43:1; 44:2). From their inception as a group, therefore, the disciples can be seen to comprise the nucleus of the end-time people of God (10:29–30; 14:58; 16:7).

Jesus chooses the twelve according to Mark in order that "they might be with him" (3:14). As those who accompany him, they become witnesses to his public ministry of teaching, preaching, and healing. As if to emphasize the notion that the disciples, as witnesses, are continually present with Jesus until the passion, Mark halts his narration of the ministry of Jesus and tells of the death of John the Baptist exactly at that point where Jesus sends the disciples on a mission that temporarily takes them away from him (cf. 6:7–13, 30 to 6:14–29). In a phrase, what Jesus entrusts to the disciples in the course of his ministry is "the mystery of the kingdom of God" (4:11). This encompasses, ultimately, the contents of Mark's Gospel. Through Jesus the disciples become the recipients of divine revelation (4:11). This means that they furthermore are regarded as the transmitters to the post-Easter church of the tradition that originates with Jesus himself.

The Marcan Jesus furthermore chooses the disciples in order that they might be his emissaries, or "apostles" (3:14–15; 6:30). He himself has been sent by God (9:37; 12:6), and he, in turn, sends them (3:14; 6:7). Their initial mission is to Israel (6:7, 12–13, 30). They are to preach repentance (3:14; 6:12), to exorcise demons (3:15; 6:7, 13), and to heal the sick (6:13), exactly as Jesus has been doing. Hence, their mission prior to Easter proves itself to be an extension of his earthly activity.

Thus far, the disciples of Jesus have been cast in a favorable light. But in three boat scenes in particular (4:35–41; 6:45–52; 8:14–21), another side of them appears. The root problem is a persistent lack of comprehension on their part (4:41; 6:52; 8:17, 21). Although entrusted with the mystery of the kingdom of God, they nevertheless fail to grasp who Jesus is (4:41). Also, by their self-concern (4:39), cowardice (4:40), fearfulness (4:41; 6:50), and astonishment (6:51), they show that they have no faith in Jesus' power to sustain them in adverse circumstances (4:40; 6:52). In short, the disciples reveal themselves in these scenes to be like the Jews "outside" (4:11–12), i.e., to be blind, deaf, and hard of heart (6:52; 8:17–18).

Nor does the ability of the disciples to comprehend Jesus improve at all after Peter correctly confesses Jesus to be the Messiah (8:29) or Peter, James, and John bear witness to his transfiguration as the Son of God (9:2–8). Indeed, they resist the cardinal truth Jesus would impress upon them, namely, that the way of the disciple is the way of suffering. Peter, for instance, following Jesus' first prediction of his passion (8:31), flatly dismisses the idea of suffering (8:32–33). Jesus counters this by declaring to the crowd and the disciples that discipleship, and in fact the attainment of salvation, involves denying oneself, taking up one's cross, and coming after him (8:34–37). Again, following Jesus' second prediction of his passion (9:31), the disciples become embroiled in a dispute over "who is the greatest" (9:34). Jesus settles this by laying down the dictum they must place at the basis of their life together: "If any one would be first, he must be last of all and servant of all" (9:35). And following Jesus' third prediction of his passion (10:32–34), the disciples fall to quarreling over the matter of status in the place of future glory (10:35–41). Jesus acquits this by citing two further dicta similar to the first: ". . . whoever would be great among you must be your

servant; and whoever would be first among you must be slave of all"
(10:43–44). Even more significantly, however, Jesus crowns his
words to them by holding up to them himself as the model they are
to emulate: "For the Son of man also came not to be served but to
serve, and to give his life as a ransom for many" (10:45).

Where the disciples' lack of comprehension finally lands them is
described by Mark in the passion account. Although they solemnly
promise that they will suffer with Jesus (14:31), Judas betrays him
(14:43–46), the other disciples abandon him and flee (14:50), and
Peter denies him (14:66–72). Nevertheless, this is not the end for
the disciples in Mark's story. In his death and resurrection, Jesus
fulfills, ironically, the prophecy that he will "build a temple not made
with hands" (14:58; 15:29). This he accomplishes through the projected fulfillment of the promise given the disciples that they will
"see" him in Galilee (14:27–28; 16:7). In Galilee, the disciples will
encounter Jesus as the crucified Son of God whom God has raised
from the dead (16:6–7). Viewing Jesus thusly in the light of the
cross, the disciples will see themselves, as his followers, as cast in
that same light. So "enlightened," they will comprehend at last that
for one truly to be Jesus' disciple, one must walk after him by taking up one's cross (8:34).

To step back for a moment and to look at the whole of Mark's
kerygmatic story, it is apparent from the preceding that this third
narrative line, which focuses on the disciples, ends exactly where the
other two narrative lines do also: at the projected meeting of the
crucified and risen Son of God with the disciples in Galilee (16:6–
7). Thus, the narrative line that can be traced through the six summary passages leads to this point, because the passion predictions all
conclude with a reference to the resurrection of Jesus (8:31; 9:31;
10:34). The narrative line along which the secret of Jesus' divine
Sonship unfolds also extends to this point, because here for the first
time the disciples are enabled to comprehend fully that Jesus is the
royal Son of God (9:7, 9–10; 14:28; 16:6–7). And the narrative
line that treats of the disciples likewise flows to this point, because
here is where the disciples become enlightened about the true meaning of following after Jesus. With these three narrative lines con-
verging in this manner on this one point, Mark deftly brings his
kerygmatic story to a well-rounded conclusion.

SOTERIOLOGY

For whom does Mark pen his kerygmatic story? Scholars agree that Mark can be thought of as writing about A.D. 70 for a community of Greek-speaking Christians. In this concluding section, we should like briefly to explore this community and its notion of salvation.

The Community of Mark

There is virtual unanimity among scholars that chap. 13 is one place where Mark has Jesus speak directly to the situation of Mark's own post-Easter community. Since, relative to the time of Mark, the ministry of Jesus lies in the past, Mark presents the earthly Jesus as addressing the future through the vehicle of prophecy (13:4).

In chap. 13, Jesus predicts the destruction of the temple (13:2). When asked by the four disciples when this will take place (13:4a–b), Jesus' reply is couched in language that seems to refer to the Jewish War and the upheavals and starvation that accompanied it (13:7–8). These passages, in turn, go with others in the Gospel that also refer to the destruction of the temple[29] or of Jerusalem (12:9). It seems likely, therefore, that by the time Mark wrote his Gospel the city and the temple had already been put to ruin. At any rate, because the impression one gets is that Mark stands close to these events, scholars generally date his Gospel about A.D. 70.

The Christians of Mark's community are apparently to be regarded as being of both Jewish and Gentile background. Factors in the Gospel that suggest this are such as the following: the great crowd that streams to Jesus and follows him comprises people from both Jewish and Gentile lands (3:7–8); Jesus feeds both the five thousand "Jews" (6:32–44) and the four thousand "Gentiles" (8:1–10); Jesus declares all foods to be clean, which opens the way for table-fellowship between Jews and Gentiles (7:14–23); the (new) covenant Jesus establishes while eating with his Jewish disciples is for Gentiles as well (14:24); and if the first human being to confess Jesus to be the Son of God is a Roman centurion (15:39), the Jewish disciples nevertheless receive the promise that they will "see" the risen Son of God in Galilee (14:27–28; 16:7).

As one might expect, this community of Jewish and Gentile Christians did not live under the jurisdiction of official Judaism. Jesus has, it believes, set aside the tradition of the elders (7:1–13). Moreover, it is his word in the last analysis, not that of Moses, that is authoritative for it, as the pronouncements of the Marcan Jesus on divorce (10:2–12) and on the cleanness of all foods (7:14–23) reveal. Then, too, the ethic of this community is, strictly speaking, geared to the will of God as mediated by Jesus (3:35; 12:28–31) and not simply to the law of Moses.

Socioculturally, the Marcan community lived in close proximity to Jews and Gentiles. It is subject to persecution at the hands of both groups.[30] As John (1:14) and Jesus (14:41–46) have been "handed over" to their enemies, so these Christians are being "handed over" (13:9, 11). Indeed, they are "hated" by both Jews and Gentiles (13:13). They are hauled before local Jewish authorities and flogged (13:9) or made to give answer to Gentile rulers (13:9), and the purpose seems clear: they should renounce their fealty to Jesus (8:34–38). In point of fact, such persecution does not exclude mutilation or martyrdom (8:34–36; 9:42–48) and occurs as the direct result of missionary activity (13:9c).

Internally, too, the community is experiencing grave difficulties. It is beset by false messiahs who, through the great signs and wonders they perform, appear to claim for themselves the authority of the risen Christ and even to assume his identity (13:6; cf. 13:21–22). These persons are "leading many astray" (13:5–6; cf. 9:42). By the same token, the evils of persecution extend even to families, as one member "delivers up to death" another (13:12; cf. 10:29). On top of these problems, there are those in the community who are also in danger of giving themselves over to the "cares of the world" and the "delight in riches" and hence of losing their faith (4:18–19; 10:23–27). And there are those, it seems, who are desirous of securing for themselves positions of status within the community (9:35; 10:35–44). The latter, judging from the space Mark devotes to combating it in the section 8:31—10:45, is an especially grievous problem.

Where is this Marcan community to be located? The answer to this question is the same as the answer to another question: Where did Mark write his Gospel? Some scholars argue for Rome,[31] whereas others argue for a region in the Near East, such as Palestine[32] or Syria.[33] At present, the evidence is not conclusive either way.

The suggestion of someplace in Syria, however, is attractive. The apparent proximity of Mark to the events of the Jewish War (13:7–8), the Semiticized flavor of much of his Greek,[34] the Jewish cast of his Christology, his attitude toward the Mosaic law and the Pharisaic tradition of the elders, and the existence of a Greek-speaking community of Jewish and Gentile Christians—all of these factors would be compatible with this area. The Latinisms of the Gospel, which tend to be of a technical and military nature,[35] could be accounted for as the influence of the Roman occupation on the culture of a subjugated land. The tendency to explain certain Semitic words (cf. 5:41; 7:34; 15:22, 34) or Jewish customs (cf. 7:3–4) could simply represent an accommodation to the Gentiles in the community. If Mark were in fact at home in Syria as opposed to Palestine, this could also explain his shaky grasp of Palestinian geography.[36] Jesus' journeys on and around the Sea of Galilee, for example, have long been the bane of geographers (cf., e.g., 6:45—7:37; esp. 7:31).

Do the Marcan Christians, like the Christians that stand behind the document of Q, form an itinerant community of prophetic-charismatic stripe?[37] It does not seem so. Methodologically, one has grounds for assuming itinerancy in the case of the community of Q, because this community sees as its mission the continuation of the preaching and the life-style of the earthly Jesus. By contrast, Mark operates with a scheme of salvation history that distinguishes between the pre-Easter mission of Jesus and the disciples and the post-Easter mission of the church (13:10; 14:9). The pre-Easter mission of the disciples terminates upon their return to Jesus (6:30). The "guidelines for itinerancy" (6:7–13) given them, therefore, cannot willy-nilly be applied to the post-Easter community of Mark. If we are to conceive of these guidelines as still being in force at the time of Mark, then perhaps they apply to the missionaries of the community.

One factor that cannot be ignored in any reconstruction of the Marcan community is the strong rural atmosphere that pervades Mark's story. Save for Jerusalem, it is not the city that is front and center, but the countryside or the "village" (cf. 1:38–39; 6:6, 56;

8:27). It is the world of the fisherman (1:16–20), the tax-collector (2:14–17), and the farmer (chap. 4).[38] Socioeconomically, the conditions described comport themselves neither with poverty nor with wealth. If Mark's Gospel can be taken as an index of the social status of the community that stands behind it, this community can be construed as being domiciled, rural, and perhaps middle-class.

The Locus of Salvation

The community of Mark knows itself to be the end-time people of God. It traces its origins to the earthly ministry of Jesus Messiah, the Son of God. It is he who has created this community (3:14, 16). He did it by calling disciples to be with him (1:16–20; 2:14; 3:13–16), by establishing the (new) covenant in pouring out his blood on the cross (14:24; cf. 10:45), and, after Easter, by reconstituting the disciples as a community by appearing to them in Galilee (14:28, 58; 15:30; 16:7). The first disciples, in being "with him" (3:14), were witnesses to his ministry and transmitters of the tradition of his words and deeds. Prior to his resurrection, they did not comprehend the revelation imparted to them. But when they "saw" him in Galilee following his resurrection (16:7), their minds were opened to perceive what previously had been withheld from them. In short, the community of Mark looks upon itself as continuing in a line with the original disciples of Jesus.

As the end-time people of God, the community of Mark understands itself to be living in the sphere of the kingdom, or rule, of God. God's end-time kingdom became a present reality in the advent of the earthly Son of God. In the post-Easter time of Mark, it continues to be a present reality (4:26–29, 30–32). It may be that the Marcan community practices the rite of "baptism" (1:8).[39] In this case, baptism is the avenue by which people enter both the circle of the community and the sphere of the kingdom. In any event, the community commemorates, through its celebration of its own "passover meal," the establishment by Jesus of the (new) covenant in his blood (14:16, 22–24). This is at the basis of the fellowship that exists in the community between Jew (6:32–44) and Gentile (8:1–10).

Living in the sphere of the kingdom, the community of Mark observes the will of God as the earthly Son of God has taught it. In faith and prayer, it enters into the presence of the risen Son of God, trusting that he will meet its needs with the same divine power with which he once expelled demons and healed the sick. This is all the more important because this community has a mission to discharge. It is to proclaim the gospel about the saving activity of God in his royal Son to all the nations (13:10; 14:9). In pursuit of this mission, the community struggles against formidable obstacles. It is persecuted from without (13:9–13; 4:17), and must contend with false messiahs and false notions of discipleship from within.[40] Still, as it pursues its mission, it presses forward in the attitude of watchful anticipation of the end (13:28–37). Eagerly it awaits the coming on the clouds in power and glory of Jesus, the transcendent Son of man (13:24–27). When he comes, he will gather all those who are his "elect" (13:27) but punish all those who have joined themselves to "this adulterous and sinful generation" (8:38; 14:62).

As one surveys Mark's scheme of salvation, it cannot be emphasized too much that the center from which the whole derives its meaning is the cross. For Mark, to live in the sphere of the eschatological kingdom is to live under the sign of the cross. The earthly Son of God whom Mark presents as teaching the will of God and performing powerful acts is at the same time the one whose ministry reaches its culmination in the cross. By the same token, the resurrected Son of God remains forever the "crucified one" (16:6). In the strictest sense, therefore, it is the will of God as taught by the crucified one that the community of Mark observes, and it is the power of the crucified one that is, through faith and prayer, available in time of need. Similarly, the gospel that the Marcan community proclaims tells of the salvation that God has effected, and continues to effect, in the crucified one. It describes the essence of true discipleship in terms of being summoned by the crucified one to take up one's own cross and to follow after. Even the persecution the community has to endure is likened to the persecution the earthly Son of God—Son of man had to endure in being "handed over" to suffer and to be crucified. Accordingly, the community of Mark vigorously pursues its mission of proclaiming the gospel to the nations in watchful anticipation of the parousia, but it does so under the sign of the cross.

NOTES

1. Cf. F. G. Lang, "Kompositionsanalyse des Markusevangeliums," *Zeitschrift für Theologie und Kirche,* 74 (1977), 1–24.
2. Cf. C. H. Talbert, *What Is a Gospel?* (Philadelphia: Fortress, 1977).
3. For a recent survey of Marcan studies, cf. J. D. Kingsbury, "The Gospel of Mark in Current Research," *Religious Studies Review,* 5 (1979), 101–7. Instructive, nontechnical studies of Mark's Gospel are the following: P. J. Achtemeier, *Mark* (Proclamation Commentaries; Philadelphia: Fortress, 1975); R. Martin, *Mark: Evangelist and Theologian* (Grand Rapids: Zondervan, 1973); and W. H. Kelber, *Mark's Story of Jesus* (Philadelphia: Fortress, 1979).
4. Cf. H.-W. Kuhn, *Aeltere Sammlungen im Markusevangelium* (SUNT 8; Göttingen: Vandenhoeck & Ruprecht, 1971).
5. It should be noted, however, that scholars agree neither as to whether a pre-Marcan passion account ever existed nor, if it be granted that one did exist, as to its length and composition.
6. A more detailed outline to which several scholars subscribe is the following: (1) The prologue (1:1–13 [15]); (2) Jesus' activity in Galilee (1:14—3:6); (3) Jesus' activity beside the sea (3:7—6:6a); (4) Jesus' activity beyond Galilee (6:6b—8:26); (5) Jesus' journey to Jerusalem (8:27—10:52); (6) Jesus' activity in Jerusalem (11:1—13:37); and (7) Jesus' passion and resurrection (14:1—16:8).
7. For a survey of the dominant approach to the Christology of Mark since the beginning of the century, cf. J. D. Kingsbury, "The 'Divine Man' as the Key to Mark's Christology—The End of an Era?" *Interpretation,* 35 (July 1981).
8. Cf. J. D. Kingsbury, "The Spirit and the Son of God in Mark's Gospel," *Sin, Salvation, and the Spirit,* ed. D. Durken (Collegeville, Minn.: Liturgical Press, 1979), pp. 195–202.
9. Cf. R. Pesch, *Das Markusevangelium* (HTKNT 2; Freiburg: Herder, 1976), 2. 179.
10. Cf. J. D. M. Derrett, "Law in the New Testament: The Palm Sunday Colt," *Novum Testamentum,* 13 (1971), 241–58.
11. Cf. G. Schneider, "Die Davidssohnfrage (Mk 12, 35–37)," *Biblica,* 53 (1970), 89–90.
12. Cf., e.g., 1 Kings 18:31; Isa. 54:11–13; Lam. 4:1–2.
13. On Mark's literary use of "prediction," cf. N. R. Petersen, *Literary Criticism for New Testament Critics* (Guides to Biblical Scholarship; Philadelphia: Fortress, 1978), chap. 3; idem, "When is the End not the End? Literary Reflections on the Ending of Mark's Narrative," *Interpretation,* 34 (1980), 151–66.
14. Cf. Mark 1:7, 14–15, 38–39; 2:17; 6:34; 12:6.
15. Cf. Mark 5:1–20; 7:24–30, 31–37; 8:1–10.
16. Cf. Mark 1:14, 39; 9:30.
17. Cf. Mark 2:1; 3:20; 7:17; 9:33.
18. Cf. Mark 1:38; 6:6b, 56; 8:22–23, 27.
19. Cf. Mark 2:13; 3:9, 20; 4:1; 5:21; 6:34; 7:14; 8:34; 9:14; 10:1, 46; 11:18; 12:12, 37.
20. Cf. also Achtemeier, *Mark,* chap. 6.
21. Cf. Mark 9:43, 45, 47; 10:23.

22. Cf. J. Behm, *"Metanoeō,"* *Theological Dictionary of the New Testament,* IV (1967), 1002.

23. Cf. also Achtemeier, *Mark,* chap. 7.

24. Cf. ibid., chap. 8.

25. Cf. Mark 1:44–45; 7:36–37; also 5:20; 7:24. Cf. further 5:43.

26. On the trial narrative in Mark, cf. J. R. Donahue, *Are You the Christ* (SBLDS 10; Missoula, Mont.: University of Montana, 1973); idem, "Temple, Trial, and Royal Christology," *The Passion in Mark,* ed. W. H. Kelber (Philadelphia: Fortress, 1976), pp. 61–79; D. Juel, *Messiah and Temple* (SBLDS 31; Missoula, Mont.: Scholars, 1977).

27. Cf., e.g., Mark 4:38; 9:5, 38; 10:35; 11:21; 13:1; also 14:14.

28. Cf. also Achtemeier, *Mark,* chap. 10.

29. Cf. Mark 11:12–21; 14:58; 15:29, 38.

30. Cf. B. M. F. van Iersel, "The gospel according to St. Mark— written for a persecuted community," *Nederlands Theologisch Tijdschrift,* 34 (1980), 15–36.

31. Cf., e.g., Pesch, *Markusevangelium,* 1. 12–13; E. Best, "The Role of the Disciples in Mark," *New Testament Studies,* 23 (1977), 379.

32. Thus, W. Marxsen (*Mark the Evangelist,* tr. R. A. Harrisville [Nashville: Abingdon, 1969], pp. 54–95) advocates Galilee, while S. Schulz (*Die Stunde der Botschaft* [Hamburg: Furche, 1967], p. 9) holds to the Decapolis.

33. Cf. H. C. Kee, *Community of the New Age: Studies in Mark's Gospel* (Philadelphia: Westminster, 1977), p. 105.

34. Cf. N. Turner, *Style,* in J. H. Moulton, *A Grammar of New Testament Greek* (Edinburgh: T. & T. Clark, 1906–1976), 4. 19.

35. Cf. W. G. Kümmel, *Introduction to the New Testament,* tr. H. C. Kee (revised ed.; Nashville: Abingdon, 1975), pp. 97–98; Turner, *Style,* pp. 29–30.

36. Cf. Kee, *Community of the New Age: Studies in Mark's Gospel,* p. 103.

37. Cf. ibid., pp. 87–105.

38. Cf. ibid., pp. 90–91.

39. Cf., e.g., V. Taylor, *The Gospel according to St. Mark* (London: Macmillan, 1952), p. 157; E. Haenchen, *Der Weg Jesu* (Berlin: Töpelmann, 1966), p. 45; Pesch, *Markusevangelium,* 1. 83.

40. Cf. Mark 4:19; 9:34–35; 10:42–45; 13:6, 12, 21–22; also 9:42.

CHAPTER THREE

MATTHEW

The emphasis in the document of Q is on the parousia. The emphasis in the Gospel of Mark is on the cross. Although the evangelist Matthew both affirms the significance of the cross and awaits the parousia, neither of these is the controlling element in his thought. Instead, central to his Gospel is the notion that God, in the person of his Son Jesus, draws near with his eschatological rule to abide with his people (1:23; 18:20; 28:20). To proclaim this truth, Matthew recasts the traditions concerning Jesus which he has inherited from both Mark and the community of Q.

THE ACCOMPLISHMENT OF MATTHEW

Most scholars remain convinced that the two-source hypothesis, whatever its limitations, accounts best for the literary relationships that obtain among the synoptic Gospels. On this view, Matthew has conjoined with one another the traditions of Mark, of Q, and of the oral or written materials peculiar to himself.

Of interest is the way in which Matthew has arranged the tradition of Mark relative to that of Q. He has, in effect, taken the Marcan tradition for his framework and expanded it by adding the tradition of Q. The upshot is that the tradition of Q, which comprises in the main sayings of Jesus, appears in the great speech-complexes of Matthew's Gospel (chaps. 5—7; 10; 13; 18; 23; 24—25). These speech-complexes, in relation to the whole of the Gospel, precede the climax, which is the story of the passion and resurrection of Jesus (chaps. 26—28). Consequently, the overall flow of Matthew's narrative is such that the Jesus who delivers the several great discourses becomes the Jesus whose career culminates in his passion and resurrection. The net result of the way in which Matthew has arranged his materials, therefore, is that he has subordinated the discourse tradition of Q to the "passion kerygma" of Mark. Hence, Matthew, in giving the nod to Mark over Q, can be seen to write a "gospel," or "kerygmatic story."

Matthew's Gospel as a Kerygmatic Story

The gospel, or kerygmatic story, Matthew pens assumes the form of a "life of Jesus." Of course, like Mark's Gospel it is no biography or literary documentary on "what really happened." But it is decidedly broader in scope than is the story of Mark. It begins, not with the baptism of Jesus, but with his genealogy, birth, and infancy (chaps. 1—2). And it concludes, not simply with the prediction that the disciples will see the risen Jesus, but with a pericope that actually tells of his appearance to them on a mountain in Galilee (28:16–20).

Matthew's "life of Jesus" unfolds according to a clear-cut topical outline. To mark off the main parts, Matthew employs a "formula," or stereotyped phrase: "From that time on Jesus began to preach [to show his disciples] . . ." (4:17; 16:21). The thing to observe is that each time this formula occurs, it introduces a new phase in the ministry of Jesus. Consequently, if it is taken as the cue, the following broad outline of Matthew's Gospel readily emerges:[1] (1) the person of Jesus Messiah (1:1—4:16); (2) the public proclamation of Jesus Messiah (4:17—16:20); and (3) the suffering, death, and resurrection of Jesus Messiah (16:21—28:20). As this outline suggests, Matthew narrates a "life of Jesus" by first presenting him to the reader and then by describing, respectively, his public ministry and his passion and resurrection.

Matthew highlights the fundamental message of his "life of Jesus" in the key passages 1:23 and 28:20. These passages stand in a reciprocal relationship to each other. At 1:23, Matthew quotes Isaiah as he says of Jesus: in "Emmanuel . . . God [is] with us." And at 28:20, the risen Jesus himself declares to his disciples: "I am with you always, to the close of the age." Strategically located at the beginning and the end of Matthew's Gospel, these two passages "enclose" it. In combination, they reveal that the message Matthew proclaims with his kerygmatic story is that in the person of Jesus Messiah, his Son, God has drawn near to abide to the end of time with his people, the church, thus inaugurating the eschatological age of salvation.

The Theological Claim of Matthew's Gospel

Matthew, no more than Mark, views Jesus in isolation from the stream of history. On the contrary, he places his story of Jesus in a setting that extends from Abraham, the father of Israel (1:2), to the consummation of the age (28:20). Still, Matthew divides this broad span of salvation history more sharply than Mark into distinct epochs and periods.

The two epochs Matthew distinguishes are the age of prophecy, or the "time of Israel (OT)," and the eschatological age of fulfillment, which is the "time of Jesus (earthly—exalted)."[2] To stress the passing of the first and the arrival of the second, Matthew makes use of numerous formula quotations that call attention to the fulfillment in the life of Jesus of some aspect of OT prophecy.[3]

For its part, the age of fulfillment, or the "time of Jesus (earthly—exalted)," runs from the birth of Jesus (1:22–23) to his parousia as the Son of man (25:31–46). Within this epoch, Matthew differentiates among several periods through his use of the respective expressions "the kingdom of Heaven is at hand" and "the gospel of the kingdom." Specifically, he employs these expressions to divide the "time of Jesus (earthly—exalted)" into the ministries to Israel of John (3:1–2), of Jesus (4:17), and of the pre-Easter disciples (10:7) and the ministry to the nations of the post-Easter disciples, or church (24:14; 26:13).

Accordingly, Matthew, more noticeably than Mark, both knits together, and differentiates among, the ministries of John, Jesus, the pre-Easter disciples, and the post-Easter church. But as with Mark, so with Matthew it is the ministry of Jesus that is decisive in this sequence. John is the forerunner of Jesus (17:10–13), and the pre-Easter and post-Easter disciples carry out their ministries only on the commission of Jesus (10:5; 28:18–20). This is why the "time of fulfillment" is indeed the "time of Jesus (earthly—exalted)."

The preceding survey of both the topical outline of Matthew's "life of Jesus" and the salvation-historical context within which he places it brings us to the question of the theological claim of his Gospel. We stated above that the passages 1:23 and 28:20 "enclose" the Gospel. As a word of prophecy, 1:23 shows that in the birth of "Emmanuel," i.e., Jesus Son of God, the hope of Israel has at last come to its fulfillment. Hence, Matthew affirms in this passage that Jesus is of decisive significance for the salvation of Israel. In 28:18–20, the risen Son of God commissions his followers to "make disciples of all the nations." Hence, Matthew affirms in this passage that Jesus is of decisive significance for the salvation of the Gentiles. Together, therefore, these passages set forth the broad theological claim Matthew advances on behalf of Jesus: for the salvation of both Jew and Gentile, Jesus Son of God is of decisive significance.

In sum, then, the accomplishment of Matthew is that he has drawn on Q, Mark, and materials peculiar to himself in order to fashion his own kerygmatic story about Jesus. He divides it into three main parts (1:1—4:16; 4:17—16:20; 16:21—28:20), and places it within the context of the history of salvation. Matthew's kerygmatic story focuses less intensely upon the cross as such than does that of Mark; this is apparent already from the fact that Matthew devotes proportionately less space than Mark to the narration of the passion of Jesus. The central message of Matthew's story is that in Jesus Messiah, his Son, God has drawn near to abide with his people and thus has inaugurated the end-time age of salvation. As it proclaims this message, Matthew's story at the same time advances the theological claim that Jesus Son of God is of ultimate importance for Jew and Gentile alike.

THE FIGURE OF JESUS[4]

The first main part of Matthew's Gospel (1:1—4:16) is not, strictly speaking, a prologue. It is, more accurately, the initial phase of the story to be narrated. The major purpose of this part of Matthew's story is to inform the reader as to who Jesus is (1:1). And because Matthew departs from Mark and tells first of the origins and infancy of Jesus, the reader is not introduced to John the Baptist until chap. 3.

Jesus as the Messiah, the Son of God

Matthew writes in the opening verse that Jesus is the "Messiah, the Son of David, the Son of Abraham" (1:1). Interestingly, Matthew omits from this pedigree his preeminent title for Jesus, that of the "Son of God." The reason is that this latter title is of such importance that Matthew will allow no one other than God himself to be the first to utter it, at Jesus' baptism (3:17).

The Matthaean Jesus, therefore, is the Davidic Messiah, the royal Son of God, who descends from Abraham. For this understanding of Jesus, Matthew is basically in debt to Mark. What Matthew has done is to adopt Mark's Christology, elaborate it, and adapt it to meet the needs of a new situation.

Matthew makes use of christological terms with great skill in order to describe the person and mission of Jesus. The very name "Jesus," for instance, means "God is salvation." Matthew plays on this meaning early in his story in order to alert the reader to the nature and scope of Jesus' mission. To Joseph the angel declares, ". . . you shall call his name 'Jesus,' for he shall save his people from their sins" (1:21). Salvation from sin, therefore, is what Jesus is about. Moreover, because the personal name "Jesus" harbors within it what Matthew takes to be Jesus' calling, he removes it from the realm of familiar usage. Thus, Bartimaeus and the two demoniacs may address Jesus by his name in Mark's Gospel (1:24; 5:7; 10:47), but Matthew erases these touches (8:29; 20:30).

Matthew's broad description of Jesus is that he is the "Messiah" (1:1, 16, 17). As the Messiah, he is the Coming One foretold by the prophets and awaited by Israel (11:2–6). Standing in the line of David (1:1, 17, 25), he brings the history of Israel to its culmination (1:1, 17). He is invested with the authority of God, and encounter with him is no idle event, for one's salvation hinges on it (3:11; 11:2–6).

Mark makes no mention of Jesus as being the "Son of Abraham." Matthew's interest in this title (1:1) is twofold. On the one hand, he is concerned to show that Jesus is the one in whom the entire history of Israel, which had its beginning in Abraham, attains to its fulfillment (1:17). On the other hand, he is concerned to present Jesus as the one in whom God makes good on the promise he gave to Abraham regarding the Gentiles (Gen. 12:3; 18:18; 22:18; 26:4). The "many" who put their faith in him, asserts the Matthaean Jesus, "will come from east and west and sit at table with Abraham, Isaac, and Jacob in the kingdom of Heaven" (8:10–11).

Of all the evangelists, none occupies himself more with the Davidic sonship of Jesus than does Matthew.[5] Whereas Mark and Luke, for example, employ the title Son of David only four times each, Matthew employs it no fewer than eleven times: ten times it refers to Jesus (cf. concordance); and once it refers to Joseph ("Joseph, son of David"; 1:20).

By and large, Matthew pursues two objectives in his use of the title Son of David. The one objective is simply to affirm the Davidic lineage of Jesus. Still, this is not without problems. The Matthaean genealogy of Jesus runs through Joseph (1:16). In Matthew's eyes, therefore, Joseph is clearly a "son of David" (1:16, 20). The problem, however, is that as Matthew presents it, Joseph is neither the physical father of Jesus (1:18, 20, 23, 25) nor does Mary stand in the line of David (1:16). This problem comes to a head in the last link of Matthew's genealogical chain: ". . . and Jacob fathered Joseph, the husband of Mary, from whom Jesus was born, who is called the Messiah" (1:16).

But if Joseph is not really the father of Jesus and his mother Mary is not from the house of David, how can Jesus legitimately be said to be the "Son of David"? In his pericope on the origin of the Messiah, Matthew gives his answer to this question (1:18–25). It is that Jesus, miraculously conceived by the Holy Spirit (1:18, 20), receives his name from Joseph (1:25). What this means, in turn, is that Matthew's solution to the problem of Jesus' genealogy is that he can legitimately be called the Son of David because Joseph son of David adopts him into his line (cf. 13:55: "Is not this the son of the carpenter?").

The second objective Matthew pursues with his Son-of-David Christology is that of focusing on the guilt that is Israel's for not receiving its Messiah. As the Son of David, Jesus is promised and sent specifically to Israel (1:1; 15:22–24; 21:5, 9; 22:42). Through individual acts of healing, he demonstrates this. These acts extend to such persons as the following: two "blind men" (9:27–31), a "blind and dumb man" (12:22), the "daughter" of a Gentile woman (15:21–28), two more "blind men" (20:29–34), and the "blind and lame" in the temple (21:14). What is noteworthy about these persons is that they are the ones who count for nothing in Israel, which is likewise true of the "children" who hail Jesus as the Son of David in the temple (21:5) and the Canaanite "woman" who pleads the cause of her daughter (15:21–22).

Now these "no-accounts," or those who assist them, acknowledge in the attitude of faith that Jesus is the Son of David. The irony is that in so doing, they "see" and "confess" what the leaders of Israel and the crowds do not. When the leaders of Israel, for example, witness the healing activity of Jesus Son of David, this only provokes them to anger (21:15) or motivates them to charge him with being an emissary of Satan (9:32–34; 12:22–24). For their part, the crowds at least pose the question as to whether Jesus is the Son of David (12:23). But the manner in which they frame it anticipates, in the Greek original, a negative reply (12:23). And when Jesus enters Jerusalem and the crowds do hail him as the Son of David, they explain that this means no more than that he is "the prophet . . . from Nazareth" (21:9–11). Consequently, by contrasting sharply the reception of Jesus as the Son of David by certain "no-accounts" with Israel's refusal to acknowledge him as such, Matthew calls attention to the guilt that accrues to Israel for its blindness.

But although Matthew strongly affirms the Davidic sonship of Jesus Messiah, Jesus is more for him than merely the Son of David. For Mark, too, of course the latter is also true. But whereas Mark does not squarely address this issue until the pericope on the question about David's son in chap. 12 (cf. Matt. 22:41–46), Matthew addresses it already in this first part of his Gospel. His theological position, like that of Mark, is that Jesus is preeminently the "Son of God." But while this title is rich in content for both Mark and Matthew, the chief emphasis is not the same. In oversimplified terms, what it says of Jesus in Mark's story is that he is the royal Messiah who dies upon the cross (14:35–36; 15:39; cf. 12:1–12; 16:6). What it says of Jesus in Matthew's story is that he is "Emmanuel," the royal Messiah in whom God draws near to abide with his people (1:23; 18:20; 28:20).

As early as 1:16, Matthew alludes to the divine sonship of Jesus.[6] He casts the verb "to be born" in the passive voice, in this way alerting the reader to special activity on the part of God: "Jesus is born [by an act of God]." This verb, in turn, points forward to the passive participle "that which is conceived" in 1:20. This, too, alludes to divine activity, and is embedded in the pericope on the origin of Jesus (1:18–25). In this pericope, Matthew states less cryptically that Mary's conception is "by the Holy Spirit" (1:18, 20), that God through the prophet discloses the true significance of the person of her son ("God with us," 1:22–23), that Mary is a "virgin" when she bears him (1:23), and that the child cannot be from Joseph because Joseph makes no attempt to have relations with Mary until after she has given birth to her son (1:25). Taken together, the intention of these terms and statements is clear: Matthew asserts that Jesus, born of Mary, is nevertheless the Son of God, for his origin is in God.

In chap. 2, Matthew continues his description of the person of Jesus. The Magi arrive in Jerusalem and ask where the newborn "King of the Jews" is to be found (2:2). Herod responds by designating this king as the "Messiah" (2:4). His mistaken notion of the Messiah, however, is that he will seize his throne (2:3, 13). By drawing on the OT, Matthew shows that the royal Messiah is destined for far greater things than merely the overthrow of Herod: he will, in fact, be the eschatological Shepherd of God's people Israel (2:6).

Now it is striking that, following 2:6, Matthew never once refers to Jesus in chap. 2 as "king" or "ruler." Instead, he refers to him consistently as "the child" and repeatedly employs the expression "the child and [with] his mother" (2:8–9, 11, 13–14, 20–21). The remarkable thing about this latter expression is that it is at once appropriate to the narrative and a means by which Matthew can speak of Jesus without giving the impression that he is the son of Joseph and hence solely the Son of David (1:20, 25). On the contrary, in that Matthew makes reference to Jesus and Mary exclusive of Joseph, he recalls the situation of chap. 1: the virgin Mary gives birth to a son who has been conceived apart from Joseph son of David by the Holy Spirit (1:18, 20, 23). Thus, it becomes plain that the purpose of the expression "the child and [with] his mother" is to remind the reader that the son of Mary is at the same time the Son of God. Consequently, the term "the child" in chap. 2 reveals itself to be a surrogate for "Son of God," and Matthew himself confirms this observation: at 2:15, he breaks his otherwise consistent use throughout 2:7–23 of the expression "the child and [with] his mother" so that none other than God, through the prophet, might call "the child" Jesus "my Son." In the last analysis, therefore, we see that "the child" whom the Magi come to Bethlehem to "worship" (2:11) as the "King of the Jews" is in fact the "Son of God," just as "the child" whom Herod plots to kill is no political throne-pretender but the eschatological Shepherd of God's people who is likewise the "Son of God."

At the beginning of chap. 3, Matthew introduces John the Baptist to his story (3:1–12). John is the forerunner of Jesus (3:1–4, 11) and he announces, much as in Mark's Gospel: "He who is coming after me is mightier than I, whose sandals I am not worthy to carry" (3:11). Indeed, this Mightier One, predicts John, will visit Israel as one who dispenses salvation and condemnation (3:11–12).

No sooner has John foretold the coming of the Mightier One than Jesus appears at the Jordan river to be baptized by John (3:13). John would "prevent" this, objecting that he has need to be baptized by Jesus (3:14). Jesus overrules John, however, declaring that "it is fitting for us to fulfill all righteousness" (3:15). Since this "confrontation" between John and Jesus is related only by Matthew, he obviously attaches special importance to it. What purpose does it serve? It shows that Jesus submits to baptism, not because he, like Israel, must repent of sin (3:2, 6), but because he is perfectly obedient to his Father's will.

The double occurrence of the expression "and behold" at 3:16 and 3:17 indicates that it is these verses that form the climax of the baptismal scene. Following Mark rather closely, Matthew, too, depicts the descent of the Holy Spirit upon Jesus and his resultant empowerment for the messianic ministry he is shortly to begin (3:16; 4:17). Because Jesus has been conceived by the Spirit, it is ruled out that his empowerment with the Spirit at his baptism should be construed as his initial endowment with the Spirit.

The second major event to occur at the baptism is that the voice calls out from heaven, "This is my beloved Son, with whom I am well-pleased" (3:17). Once again, this declaration is a composite quotation (cf. Mark 1:11) with the words taken from Gen. 22:2, Ps. 2:7, and Isa. 42:1. They characterize Jesus as the unique Son of God from the house of David whom God has chosen for eschatological ministry in Israel.

In this declaration of the heavenly voice at 3:17, we have reached the apex, not only of the baptismal pericope, but also of the entire first main part of Matthew's story (1:1—4:16). In this part, Matthew describes the person and origins of Jesus. The overriding

1:1 — 4:16

truth he promulgates is that Jesus is the Davidic Messiah, the royal
Son of God. He does not state the whole of this truth in 1:1, the
heading of the first main part of his story. For, as something that
can be known solely by revelation (16:16–17), this truth must first
be proclaimed, not by any character in the story, but only by God.
Accordingly, Matthew alludes to this truth with circumlocutions
(1:16, 18, 20), with metaphors (2:8–9, 11, 13–14, 20–21; 3:11), or
with a term ("son") that is susceptible to dual meaning (1:21, 23,
25). He even permits it to sound softly as the word of the Lord
spoken through the prophet (1:22–23; 2:15). Still, all remains
adumbration until that climactic point following the baptism of Jesus
when the voice from heaven proclaims in the presence of John that
Jesus is indeed the unique Son of God (3:17).

The pericope on the temptation of Jesus (4:1–11) follows that
on the baptism. Because we shall discuss it later, we wish merely to
call attention here to the fact that in this passage, too, Jesus stands
forth as the "Son of God" (4:3, 6). By resisting Satan, Jesus Son
of God gives further proof of his perfect obedience to the will of
God.

By way of presenting a summary sketch of the Christology of
1:1—4:16, it is instructive to draw together the contents of several
key passages in which Matthew employs a series of related idioms.
These idioms are the following: "his people" (1:21), "my people"
(2:6), "my Son" (2:15; 3:17), and "the Son of God" (4:3, 6). In
combination, the passages containing these idioms cast Jesus in the
following light: Jesus, in the line of David (1:21), is the Son of God
(2:15; 3:17), i.e., he has his origin in God (1:20) and is the one
chosen to shepherd the end-time people of God (2:6); empowered
by God for messianic ministry (3:16–17), he proves himself in confrontation with Satan to be perfectly obedient to the will of God
(4:1–12); as such a one, he saves his (God's) people from their sins
(1:21). Although there are details still to be added, this sketch cap-
tures well Matthew's basic understanding of Jesus.

Jesus as the Son of Man[7]

Matthew has taken over Son-of-man references from both the
Marcan tradition and Q. But although Q tells of the "earthly activity" and of the "future coming" of Jesus Son of man, it is silent

concerning his "suffering." Mark, on the other hand, ascribes all three phases of activity to Jesus Son of man. Structurally, Matthew elaborates the pattern of Mark but, like Q, lays great stress on the parousia of the Son of man.[8]

To get at the function of the title Son of man in Matthew's Gospel, it is helpful to compare it with the way in which he uses the title Son of God. "Son of God" for Matthew is of the nature of a "confessional" title. Although supernatural beings, such as God (3:17; 17:5), Satan (4:3, 6), and demons (8:29), know that Jesus is the Messiah Son of God, such knowledge is beyond the natural capacity of human beings. To be sure, human beings in Matthew's story do address Jesus as the Son of God, but it is in the spirit of mockery or blasphemy (26:63; 27:40, 43). To confess Jesus to be the Son of God aright, i.e., in faith, is possible only through the gift of divine revelation (11:25-27; 13:11; 16:16-17; 27:54). To dispel any doubt about this, Matthew brings a passage not found elsewhere in the synoptic traditions. In direct response to Peter's confession, "You are the Messiah, the Son of the living God!" (16:16), the Matthaean Jesus declares: ". . . flesh and blood has not revealed this to you, but my Father who is in heaven!" (16:17). Consequently, Son of God functions as a "confessional" title in Matthew's story in the sense that the only human beings who can utter it aright are those who have been blessed by God with the "eyes of faith" (11:25; 13:16-17). The truth that this title conveys, namely, that in Jesus God is present among people with his end-time rule (1:23), is inaccessible to the "world," Jew or Gentile (11:25-27; 13:11).

Once this is understood, we can further understand how it is that Matthew handles Mark's secret of the divine sonship of Jesus. In Mark's story, the secret that Jesus is the Son of God remains in force until Jesus dies on the cross (15:39) and is raised (16:6-7). Indeed, the disciples do not comprehend this secret until they "see" Jesus in Galilee (14:28; 16:6-7). In Mark's scheme of things, it is this "seeing" of the crucified and resurrected Son of God that belongs, along with other events (3:13-16; 14:58; 15:29, 38), to the founding of the church. In Matthew's story, on the other hand, the church is founded by Jesus already during his earthly ministry (16:17-19; 18:15-20). The disciples "see" and "worship" Jesus as the Son of God before he ever dies on the cross (14:33; 16:15-16). Hence, in

Matthew's story the secret of the divine sonship of Jesus, while hidden from Israel and the world, is "given" to the disciples (11:25–27; 13:11, 16–17).

It is against this backdrop that Matthew develops his use of the title Son of man. In his Gospel as in Mark's, Jesus is never confessed to be the Son of man or even addressed as such. Accordingly, Son of man is not, like Son of God, a confessional title. On the contrary, it is what may be termed a "public" title. Indeed, the groundwork for treating it as such is present already in Mark (cf. esp. 2:6, 10, 24, 28). But in what sense is Son of man a "public" title? In the sense that it is the title by which the Matthaean Jesus refers to himself as he interacts with the "world," both Israel and the Gentiles.

Thus, the title Son of man occurs on the lips of the Matthaean Jesus in all of the following contexts: when he makes reference to himself in the audience of the Jewish crowds or of his opponents during his public ministry to Israel;[9] when he tells his disciples, in sayings like the passion predictions, about the suffering God has ordained that Judas, the Israelite leaders, and Gentiles should inflict upon him;[10] when he points to himself, in contrast to the "rulers of the Gentiles" and the "great men" of the world, as the model of self-sacrificial service his disciples are to emulate in their own lives in the world (20:25–28); when he describes himself following Easter as the Exalted One who will reign over the world and raise up in it sons of the kingdom (13:37–38); and when he sketches for the disciples his future return in glory as Judge of all the nations of the world.[11]

One passage that indicates particularly well how Matthew works with the title of Son of man is 16:13–20 (cf. also 8:19–22; 13:37–38; 26:20–25). Here Jesus asks with a view to the public, "Who do *men* say that the *Son of man* is?" (16:13). But with a view to his disciples he asks, "Who do *you* say that *I* am [= the Son of God]?" (16:15–16). The thing to observe is that whereas "Son of man" is made to correlate with "men," "I" ("Son of God") is made to correlate with the disciples. If Jesus stands before the world as the Son of man, he is known and confessed by his disciples (and church) to be the Son of God. If Son of man is a "public" title, Son of God is a "confessional" title.

Does this mean, then, that Matthew has two christological "lines" running through his Gospel which nowhere meet? No, for there is one point at which the two lines can be seen to converge: at the parousia. Mark hints of this already in his presentation (cf. 8:38), and Matthew picks up on this and develops it. In his pericope on the last judgment (25:31–46), Matthew plainly assimilates the figure of the future Son of man to the figure of the Messiah Son of God. For example, if the Messiah Son of God is a royal figure, so is the future Son of man, for Matthew terms him the "King" (25:34, 40). If the Messiah Son of God is the agent of God's eschatological kingdom (4:17; 11:2–5, 25–27; 12:28), so is the future Son of man (7:21–23; 16:27–28). If the Messiah Son of God knows God as "my Father" (11:27; 16:17), so does the future Son of man (25:34; cf. 16:27). And just as the Messiah Son of God refers to his disciples as "my brothers" (12:48–50; 28:10), so the future Son of man refers to the righteous at the latter day as "my brothers" (25:40; cf. with 18:6). Clearly, therefore, Matthew desires to show that also at his parousia as the glorious Son of man, Jesus remains the Son of God.

Matthew's view, then, is that if Jesus is known by his disciples during his ministry and by his church following Easter as the Messiah, the Son of God, he interacts with the world, first Israel and then the Gentiles, as the Son of man. At the consummation of the age, however, Jesus will appear visibly as the Judge and Ruler of the universe. At that time, the whole world will see what until then only the eyes of faith had ever been given by God to perceive: that in Jesus, God is present with his end-time rule. Consequently, at the parousia both the church and the world will behold Jesus in all the majesty of God as the Son of man. Yet, even as he appears in splendor as the Son of man, Jesus remains the Son of God, the King through whom God exercises his rule.

THE MISSION OF JESUS

Preliminary to the public ministry of Jesus in Mark's Gospel are the ministry of John the Baptist and the baptism and the temptation of Jesus. Matthew follows Mark and also treats these events as preliminary to the public ministry of Jesus (cf. 3:1—4:16 to Mark 1:2–13). In fact, Matthew shapes them so that they play a critical role in preparing the reader to understand properly the further development of his story (4:17—16:20; 16:21—28:20).

The ministry of John paves the way for the ministry of Jesus in that John readies Israel for the coming of Jesus, the Messiah Son of God (3:3, 5–6, 11–12). John is a prophet who is likewise "more than a prophet", because he is Elijah redivivus, the "forerunner" of the Messiah (11:9–10, 14). He appears in the desert of Judea and fulfills his mission by calling Israel to repentance (3:1–2, 5–6, 11). He announces the nearness of the kingdom even before Jesus does (3:1–2; 4:17), but the burden of his announcement is not of the nature of good news but of judgment (cf. 3:7–12 with 4:23). People from all the surrounding country go out to John, and they respond to his call by submitting to his baptism and confessing their sins (3:5–6). The leaders of Israel also come out to him, but for them John has only harsh words: he denounces them as a "brood of vipers" (3:7), warns them of impending judgment (3:7), enjoins them to lead lives befitting repentance (3:8), discounts their belief that they can rely for salvation on their descendency from Abraham (3:9), and predicts the imminent coming of the "Mightier One" who will exercise judgment to salvation or damnation (3:11–12).

John's prediction about the Mightier One comes true as Jesus suddenly arrives on the scene (3:13). Jesus compels John to baptize him (3:15), but not as one who must repent of sin. On the contrary, Jesus insists that he be baptized because he knows that this is God's will and he will do it (3:15). After he has been baptized, God empowers Jesus with his Spirit for messianic ministry (3:16) and declares him to be his unique Son (3:17).

Accordingly, the perception the reader has of Matthew's Jesus following the baptismal scene is that he is the Spirit-endowed Son of God who knows and does his Father's will.[12] Matthew employs the pericope on the temptation (4:1–11) to confirm this perception. The Spirit with which Jesus has been empowered leads him out into the desert to confront Satan in the place of his abode (4:1). Satan's objective is to put Jesus at cross-purposes with the will of God. He tempts Jesus (a) to rebel against God by miraculously stilling his hunger and thus forcing a change in his circumstances (4:2–4), (b) to put God to the test to see whether he will stand by his promise to protect him from harm (4:5–7), and (c) to give to him, Satan, the fealty that otherwise belongs to God (4:8–10). These temptations are all antitypical to those experienced by Israel in its wanderings in the desert (Deut. 8:3; 6:13–14, 16). But whereas Israel son of God broke faith with God, Jesus Son of God remains loyal to God. He demonstrates that he is in truth the Son who knows and does his Father's will.

This brings us to the point toward which we have been steering. The Jesus who sets out on his public ministry to Israel (4:17) is the royal Son of God who perfectly knows and does the will of God. Throughout the rest of his story (4:17—28:20), Matthew elaborates the two sides of this view of Jesus. On the one hand, Jesus is the Son who "does" the will of God. What such doing of the will of God entails Matthew brings to light in the narrative line of his story. In the second main part of his story, which is devoted to Jesus' public ministry (4:17—16:20), it entails teaching, preaching, and healing (4:23; 9:35; 11:1). In the third main part, which is devoted to Jesus' passion and resurrection (16:21—28:20), it entails submitting to betrayal, suffering, and death (16:21; 17:22-23; 20:18-19).

On the other hand, Jesus is likewise the Son who "knows" the will of God. It is in the great discourses that Matthew plays up this side of his understanding of Jesus. These discourses deal with topics that are of fundamental significance to the life of discipleship. In them, Jesus Son of God addresses himself to such matters as the ethics of the kingdom (chaps. 5—7), instructions on missionary outreach (chap. 10), secret knowledge about the kingdom (chap. 13), community life (chap. 18), and the time before the end (chaps. 24—25).

Consequently, Matthew places both the narrative line of his story and the great discourses in the service of the image he projects of Jesus at his baptism and temptation as the authoritative Son who knows and does his Father's will. In addition, however, Matthew also conveys this image of Jesus in another, more subtle, way. As compared with Mark, he intensifies the "aura of the divine" that surrounds Jesus and hence tends to clothe the earthly Jesus in the splendor of the risen Jesus his church worships and confesses.

To illustrate this, consider the term "Father." For his part, the Marcan Jesus invokes the image of God as Father only sparingly,[13] and seems not to use the expression "my Father" (but cf. 14:36). By contrast, the Matthaean Jesus makes frequent references to God as Father (cf. concordance). Not only this, but he also rigidly distinguishes in his use of this term between himself and his disciples: he speaks of "my Father" or "your Father" but never of "our Father" (the Lord's Prayer is no exception; cf. 6:9).

Other examples of this art of writing are likewise ready to hand. Thus, in forty-nine instances Matthew utilizes the verb *proserchomai* ("to come to," "to approach"), which in the LXX is cultic in coloration and in Josephus is used of stepping before a king,[14] in order to portray persons as approaching Jesus with the same reverence that would be due to a deity or king. In similar fashion, he likewise utilizes the verb *proskyneō* ("to worship," "to do obeisance to") in order to show that Jesus is the worthy object of worship.[15] In the same vein, Matthew furthermore "spiritualizes" the person of Jesus. One way he does this is by dropping Marcan references to the "feelings" of Jesus: "anger" (Mark 3:5), "pity" (Mark 1:41), "wonder" (Mark 6:6), "pneumatic frenzy" (Mark 8:12), "indignation" (Mark 10:14), and "love" (Mark 10:21). Another way he does this is by "editing out" a number of queries Jesus poses in Mark's Gospel which, on the surface, seem to intimate a lack of knowledge or perception on Jesus' part.[16] And fourth, Matthew heightens the majesty of Jesus by also modifying or omitting Marcan expressions that appear to circumscribe his authority or allude to the fact that some desire of his went unfulfilled.[17]

A special example of Matthew's penchant for coloring the earthly Jesus in the hues of the heavenly Jesus concerns the manner in which persons address Jesus. On the one hand, Matthew depicts a nonbeliever, opponents, and Judas as addressing Jesus as "teacher" or "rabbi," i.e., with terms which attribute to him human respect.[18] On the other hand, he consistently depicts the (true) disciples and those who come to Jesus in the attitude of faith as addressing him as "Lord."[19] The force of the latter title in Matthew's Gospel is such that it attributes to Jesus an exalted station and divine authority.[20]

On balance, then, if it cannot be said of Mark that he replicates in his story the historical Jesus, even less can this be said of Matthew. Quite the opposite, Matthew's goal is to make the Jesus of his story "transparent" to the Christians of A.D. 90 for whom he is writing. Hence, Matthew's Jesus is Jesus as he is known by the post-Easter church. As we mentioned above, he moves and speaks and acts with the "aura of the divine" about him.

With this image in mind of Jesus as the authoritative Son who knows and does his Father's will, we now want to look more closely at the public ministry of Jesus. This spans the second main part of Matthew's story (4:17—16:20). In three summary passages, Matthew describes the heart of it: Jesus goes "about all Galilee, teaching in their synagogues and preaching the gospel of the kingdom and healing every disease and every infirmity among the people" (4:23; 9:35; 11:1). At the same time, Matthew stresses more emphatically than Mark that Israel is the primary object of Jesus' attention. At 15:24, Jesus states categorically: "I have not been sent except to the lost sheep of the house of Israel." Similarly, Jesus commands the pre-Easter disciples with an eye to their mission: "Go nowhere among the Gentiles, and enter no town of the Samaritans, but go rather to the lost sheep of the house of Israel" (10:5–6).

To reinforce the notion that Jesus directs his activity first of all to Israel, Matthew restricts geographically the movement of Jesus. Except for brief excursions,[21] Jesus stays within the confines of Israel. Galilee is the area where he works (4:23; 9:35; 11:1) and, within Galilee, Capernaum stands out as the place in and around which numerous events of his ministry occur (cf. chaps. 8—9). Although neither Mark nor Luke ever writes that Jesus takes up residence anywhere, Matthew speaks of him as "dwelling" there (4:13). Capernaum is "his own city" (9:11), and it may be that the "house" there is to be thought of as belonging to him (cf. 9:10, 28; 12:46 and 13:1; 13:36; 17:25).

In comparison with Mark, it is with relative ease that one can also track the movement of Jesus during his public ministry in Matthew's story (4:17—16:20). This movement is without the air of haste and, at times, even aimlessness which seems to attend it in Mark's story. Thus, as the Son who knows and does his Father's will (3:13—4:11), Matthew's Jesus presents himself to Israel (4:17). He preaches to the people and summons them to repentance in view of the gracious nearness of the kingdom of heaven (4:17). He also calls his first disciples (4:18–22). Followed by them and attracting huge crowds (4:23–25; 5:1), he ascends a mountain and there teaches the will of God (5:1—7:29). Then, wandering in the area of Capernaum and traveling across the sea of Galilee and back, he performs ten mighty acts of deliverance, in so doing setting forth the nature and the cost of discipleship (8:1—9:34). At the height of his activity, he commissions the twelve to a ministry in Israel modeled on his own, one of preaching and healing though not of teaching (9:35—10:42).

Despite Jesus' ministry of teaching, preaching, and healing, however, he is repudiated as the Messiah by all segments of Israel (11: 2—12:50). Even his family appears to desert him, so that his disciples alone remain as those who are his true relatives (12:46–50). Jesus' response to this total rejection by Israel is a dual one. On the one hand, he declares that Israel has become hard of heart, and gives public demonstration of this by addressing the crowds in "parables,"[22] in speech they cannot comprehend (13:1–35). On the other hand, he turns his attention to his disciples and reveals to them the mysteries of the kingdom of heaven (13:11, 36–52). Still, by the end of Jesus' parable discourse the trend of events is clear. Because violence threatens him before "his hour" (12:14; 14:1–12), he momentarily withdraws to a deserted place (14:13) or into the regions of Tyre and Sidon (15:21) to avoid his opponents (16:4). The bright spot is that his disciples comprehend that he is in fact Israel's Messiah, the Son of God (14:33), and at the close of this phase of his activity Peter boldly confesses him to be such (16:16).

Jesus' Ministry of Preaching

Jesus' initial act as he undertakes his public ministry in Matthew's story is to proclaim, "Repent, for the kingdom of heaven is at hand" (4:17). In the three passages that summarize Jesus' activity in Israel, Matthew characterizes his message as "the gospel of the kingdom" (4:23; 9:35; [11:1]).

The term "gospel" in this expression denotes "good news." The term "kingdom" is short for the "kingdom of heaven." Hence, the message Jesus preaches in Israel is the "good news about the kingdom of heaven."

The "kingdom of heaven" is an equivalent term for the "kingdom of God." Both refer to the eschatological, or end-time, rule of God. For Matthew as for Mark, Jesus Messiah, the Son of God, is the agent of God's end-time rule (4:17; 11:25–27). Therefore in him (1:23), in his words and deeds (11:2–6), the rule of God has drawn so near (4:17) that it impinges upon the present and can be described by Matthew as a present reality (11:12; 12:28). This is the import of a saying of Jesus such as this: "But if it is by the Spirit of God that I cast out demons, then the kingdom of God has come upon you" (12:28).

As a present reality, however, the kingdom is also a hidden reality. In fact, only the followers of Jesus can perceive its presence in him. This is the truth to which the Matthaean Jesus alludes when he declares to his disciples: "But blessed are your eyes, for they see, and your ears, for they hear" (13:16).

In Matthew's thought as in Mark's, the kingdom is not only a present, hidden reality, it is also a future reality. Although it is so near that people confront it even now in Jesus Son of God, it has not yet been consummated. Indeed, Matthew depicts in some detail the future appearance of the kingdom: the Son of man will come suddenly, all the nations will be gathered before him, he will separate them into two groups, and he will speak judgment on them, thus determining who will "inherit the kingdom" and who will "go away into eternal punishment" (25:31–46; 13:40–43; 24:29–31).

Like Mark, Matthew, too, posits continuity between the present, hidden beginnings of the kingdom in the person and ministry of Jesus Son of God and the future manifestation of the kingdom in splendor at the coming of Jesus Son of man. The former will issue ineluctably in the latter (13:31–32, 33). On the other hand, Matthew possesses a more highly developed sense of the delay of the parousia of the Son of man than does Mark. To be sure, Mark affirms that "the gospel must first be preached to all nations" before the end will come (13:10; cf. 13:34). But in the parable of the talents, for example, Matthew speaks of the "lord of those slaves" as not returning until "after a long time" has passed (25:19). What this suggests is that the question of Christian existence within the world is a more insistent problem for Matthew.

In the light of Matthew's concept of the kingdom of heaven, how, then, is the expression "the gospel of the kingdom" to be defined? It is the good news that God, in the person of his Son Jesus and in the word his followers preach about him (4:23; 24:14; 26:13), has drawn near to people (first Israel and then the Gentiles) with his eschatological rule to save.

As Jesus preaches the gospel of the kingdom in Israel, he is at the same time calling people to repentance (4:17). He is, in effect, impelling them to turn away from evil and to turn toward God, i.e., to enter into the sphere of God's gracious rule by becoming his disciples (cf. 19:21). The alternative is to refuse repentance and hence to live in the sphere of Satan's rule (12:26; 13:38–39). The decision each person makes is of ultimate consequence, for it will be ratified to salvation or damnation at the latter day (11:20–24; 13:36–43).

Jesus' Ministry of Teaching

Since Matthew presents Jesus in his Gospel as the Son of God who knows and does his Father's will (3:13—4:11), it is not surprising that "teaching" should be the principal activity in which Jesus engages during his public ministry to Israel. This emphasis on teaching comes to the fore in three ways in particular. First, Matthew cites "teaching" ahead of "preaching" and "healing" in the three summary passages that describe what Jesus is about in his public ministry (4:23; 9:35; 11:1). Second, although Matthew writes that John the Baptist and the disciples "preach" (3:1; 10:7), "teaching" remains the special prerogative of Jesus (28:20). And third, Matthew has Jesus state unequivocally that he, the Messiah, is the "one teacher" of the disciples (23:8, 10).

In view of the high esteem in which Matthew holds Jesus' activity of teaching, it is ostensibly an anomaly that only a stranger, opponents, and Judas, but never the (true) disciples, address Jesus as "teacher." We recall that in Mark's Gospel the disciples do address Jesus as "teacher." But "teacher" is merely a term of human respect. For this reason, Matthew puts it on the lips of "outsiders" but replaces it with "Lord" when it comes to the disciples or to persons who approach Jesus in faith.[23] "Lord" attributes to Jesus divine authority; it is appropriate to Matthew's heightened Christology, for as the Messiah Son of God, it is with divine authority that he teaches.

Unquestionably, Mark presents Jesus, in his capacity as teacher, as the authoritative interpreter of the will of God. Still, he does not go out of his way to pit Jesus against Moses. By contrast, Matthew makes it a point to show that Jesus supersedes Moses.[24] Two examples demonstrate this. In the first place, Jesus Son of God ascends the mountain, just as Moses once ascended Mount Sinai (Exod. 24), in order to expound the will of God to the Israelite crowds and his disciples (5:1–2). In the course of his teaching, he makes prominent use of the literary device of the antithesis: "You have heard that it was said to the men of old . . . but I say to you" (5:21–22, 27–28,

31–32, 33–34, 38–39, 43–44). In so doing, Jesus reveals that it is, in principle, his word that has replaced the word of Moses. Indeed, this supersession of Moses' word by Jesus' word is also graphically illustrated at the end of the Gospel: on the mountain in Galilee, the risen Son of God enjoins his disciples to "observe all that *I* have commanded you" (28:20). And in the second place, in debates between Jesus and the Israelite leaders over matters of law, Matthew diverges from Mark and accentuates the fact that Jesus speaks the mind not merely of Moses, but of God (cf. 15:4 with Mark 7:10; 19:4 with Mark 10:3; 22:31 with Mark 12:26).

Jesus Son of God, therefore, is in Matthew's eyes the spokesman of God in a direct and immediate fashion (11:27; 28:18). He makes known the will of God in terms of its original intention (19:4, 8). With absolute sovereignty, he abrogates commands of Moses, such as those on divorce (5:31–32), oaths (5:33–37), and retribution (5:38–42).[25] Or he radicalizes commands of Moses, such as those on murder (5:21–26), adultery (5:27–30), and love of one's enemy (5:43–48). Or he repudiates demands for a false observance of commands of Moses, such as is the case with his rulings on the sabbath law (12:1–8, 9–14) and the dietary laws (15:10–20a).

By the same token, the Matthaean Jesus can also come out against the regulations of the Pharisaic "tradition of the elders" (16:11–12). He castigates, for instance, contemporary practice relative to the so-called vow of Corban (15:5–7), and he judges that "to eat with unwashed hands does not defile a person" (15:20). Or he can turn around and endorse certain of these regulations (cf. 23:2–3), as when he says of the rule concerning the tithing of mint and dill and cummin that these things ought to be done (23:23).

On the basis of these examples, it is not difficult to discern the salvation-historical principle that informs Matthew's treatment of the law. This principle is that it is in Jesus Son of God that the law, as the expression of the will of God, attains to its "fulfillment" (5:17; 11:13); it is his word that gives the law its final shape and meaning (22:16; 7:28–29). But if this is true, then it also follows that his sayings are binding on the disciples for all time to come (28:20) and will never pass away (24:35).

Does all of this mean, then, that what the Matthaean Jesus entrusts to his disciples is an elaborate system of casuistry? Certainly not. For what precludes this is the recurring insistence that the deepest intention of the will of God is love (7:12; 9:13; 12:7; 19:19): love toward God and love toward the neighbor (22:34–40). Thus, doing the will of God or keeping the injunctions of the law is in essence, Matthew maintains, always an exercise in love.

If Mark's Jesus clashes with the leaders of Israel over his interpretation of the law, the dispute between Matthew's Jesus and Israel's leaders is even more acrimonious. There is no chapter in Mark's Gospel, for example, to compare to that of Matthew 23.[26] In Matthew's perspective, the nub of the matter is that Israel's leaders prove themselves to be "hypocrites," i.e., "they preach, but they do not practice" (23:3, 13, 15, 23, 25, 27, 29). What makes this accusation so onerous is the circumstance that hypocrisy is indicative of "divided allegiance," of not being "perfect," or wholehearted in the knowledge and service of God (5:48; Deut. 18:13). Hypocrisy is, in short, "lawlessness" (23:28), which Jesus Son of man will condemn at the final judgment (13:41–43).

Jesus' Ministry of Healing

The third major facet of Jesus' public ministry in Israel is that of "healing" (4:23; 9:35; 11:1, 5).[27] Up to a point, Matthew's approach to the healing ministry of Jesus parallels that of Mark.

Like Mark, Matthew designates the miracles Jesus performs as "powerful acts" (cf. 11:20, 21, 23; 13:54; 14:2). This very term (*dynameis*) indicates that the divine authority which marks Jesus' teaching and preaching is likewise present in his deeds (cf. 21:14–15 to 21:23). As for "signs and wonders," Matthew does not associate them with Jesus. On the contrary, only "an evil and adulterous generation seeks for a sign" (12:39; 16:4), and it is the "false prophets" who do "great signs and wonders" (24:24).

Like Mark, Matthew, too, sees in the powerful acts of Jesus the cosmic struggle between the kingdom of God and the kingdom of Satan (12:24–29). Disease in people and upheaval in nature are symptoms of sin and of bondage to Satan. Hence, through the activity of healing and of exercising dominion over nature, Jesus Son of God is liberating people from the sphere of Satan's rule and bringing them into the gracious sphere of the rule of God. "But if it is by the Spirit of God that I cast out demons," Jesus proclaims, "then the kingdom of God has come upon you!" (12:28).

But there is one respect in which Matthew's portrayal of the healing activity of Jesus differs noticeably from that of Mark. For his part, Mark predicates the verb "to heal" (*therapeuō*) to Jesus only four times. Matthew, on the other hand, does so some twelve or thirteen times.[28] Now the root meaning of *therapeuō* is "to serve," and "to heal" is secondary to this. Moreover, at 8:16–17 Matthew employs a formula quotation in order to characterize the healing ministry of Jesus as the "fulfillment" of OT prophecy. Significantly, the OT passage he cites is Isa. 53:4, a verse of one of the Servant Songs: "He took our sicknesses and bore our diseases" (8:17). Taken together, these factors explain why it is that Matthew exhibits such fondness for the verb *therapeuō*: he plays on the double meaning of "to serve" and "to heal" in order to present the "healing activity" of Jesus as the "ministry of service" which the Messiah Son of God carries out on behalf of his people Israel. Jesus, therefore, "heals" the sick among the crowds and so "serves" the people of Israel by bestowing on them the blessings of the end-time rule of God.[29] Once again, therefore, Jesus sovereignly stands forth as the Son who knows and does his Father's will.

Because Jesus Son of God proffers salvation to Israel through his ministry of healing, his powerful acts, no less than his preaching, summon Israel to repentance and to discipleship (11:20–24). Israel, however, refuses such repentance (11:20). This, in turn, evokes from Jesus the stark word of judgment: "But I tell you that it shall be more tolerable on the day of judgment for the land of Sodom than for you" (11:24; cf. 11:22).

Jesus' Passion and Resurrection

· Matthew devotes the third main part of his story to the suffering, death, and resurrection of Jesus Messiah (16:21—28:20). By and large, he adheres to Mark in this part, and the three summary passages that guide the narrative are the passion predictions (16:21; 17:22–23; 20:18–19). Of immediate interest are the several themes that distinguish Matthew's version of the passion and resurrection. They contribute materially to his overall picture of Jesus as the Son who knows and does his Father's will.

To begin with, Matthew is intent, in writing of Jesus' passion, to depict him as being in complete control of the events that bring him to the cross. On the one hand, Jesus knows from the outset that at the passover Judas will betray him (26:2, 21, 25), Peter will deny him (26:34), and all the disciples will forsake him (26:31, 56). On the other hand, he has awesome, supernatural power at his disposal which he chooses not to invoke: "Do you think that I cannot appeal to my Father, and he will at once send me more than twelve legions of angels?" (26:53).

For another thing, Matthew never tires of reiterating that it is the chief priests and the elders of the people who are responsible for the death of Jesus (26:3-5, 14-15, 47, 59-66; 27:1-2). They enlist the support of Pilate and the Jewish crowds (27:2, 20-26). As for Jesus, he is the "righteous one" who is "innocent" of either blaspheming God or of fomenting insurrection against the state (26:59-60; 27:4, 18, 19, 24).

Again, Matthew makes it eminently clear exactly why it is that Jesus embraces the "sorrowful" way of the cross (26:37-38). It is not because martyrdom per se is to be sought. Rather, it is because he, the Son of God, submits his wish to have the "cup" of suffering removed from him to the will of God, his Father, that he should "drink" it (26:39, 42, 44, 54).

In other respects, Matthew also laces with irony his portrayal of Jesus' condemnation to death at his trial before the Sanhedrin (26:57-68). As things unfold, Jesus is condemned to death because he does not disclaim for himself the very truth that touches on the deepest mystery of his person: that he is in fact the Messiah, the Son of God (26:59-66).

Furthermore, Matthew construes the first half of the crucifixion scene, in line with Ps. 22 and Wisd. of Sol. 2, as a test (27:38-44). He has the passersby tempt Jesus along the same lines, and even in part with the same words, as Satan had done earlier: "If you are the Son of God, then come down from the cross" (27:40). Jesus, however, resists the temptation and commits his cause wholly to God (27:43).

Last, Matthew describes God, in immediate response to the death of Jesus, as himself attesting to the truth that Jesus is his Son. He causes supernatural portents to occur which then serve, as "revelatory events," to elicit from the Roman soldiers the confession: "Truly this man was the Son of God" (27:51–54). In other words, the confession of the Roman soldiers is at once their word and a word from God.

But this now raises the question: What is the main purpose of Jesus' death on the cross? Matthew's answer is not unlike that of Mark: atonement for sin. In fact, from the beginning of his story Matthew has been pursuing this point. In chap. 1, he alerts the reader to the circumstance that the son of Mary, who is at the same time the Son of God ("Emmanuel"), will "save his people from their sins" (1:21, 23). In the pericope on the celebration of the passover, he expands this thought to include the notion that the atonement Jesus will make will have universal efficacy: ". . . this is my blood of the covenant, which is poured out *for many* for the forgiveness of sins" (26:28). And finally, upon the death of Jesus Matthew writes that the curtain of the temple is torn in two (27:51). In Matthew's purview, this is a sign from God that the cult of Israel has been set aside and replaced by his Son, who has made final atonement for sin. Access to God is through the Son of God.

This leaves the resurrection. In Matthew's story the resurrection signifies vindication for Jesus and the commission to a new ministry for the disciples. Mark's Gospel concludes on the note that the disciples will see Jesus in Galilee (16:7). Although Mark narrates no such scene, Matthew does (28:16–20). In it, Matthew explains what it means for the "rejected stone," God's Son, to be vindicated by being placed at the "head of the corner" (21:37–38, 42). God entrusts his Son, whom he has resurrected from the dead, with all authority in heaven and on earth, i.e., he gives him rule over all (28:18). By virtue of this universal authority, the Son of God commissions his disciples to a ministry under his guiding presence which has as its goal making disciples of all the nations (28:19–20).

DISCIPLESHIP

Matthew affirms, as we mentioned above, that God is the Father of Jesus in a way that is not predicated of other human beings (11:27). Conversely, he insists that Jesus is the Son of God in a manner that is true of no one else (1:23; 3:17; 11:27).

When Jesus authoritatively summons persons to follow him and they obey his call (4:18–22; 9:9), Matthew pictures them as entering the sphere where God's end-time rule already impinges upon the present order of things (5:3–11; 11:3–5; 12:28). Through Jesus, the Messiah Son of God, these persons enter into a relationship of sonship with God. So it is that Jesus designates them as "sons of God" (5:9, 45; 13:38) and speaks to them of God as "your Father" (cf., e.g., 5:16, 45).

Although Jesus and his disciples are active in the midst of Israel, Matthew marks them off more sharply as a separate group than either Mark or Luke. Jesus is "with them" and they are "with him," and the rubric obtains: "He who is not *with me* is against me, and he who does not gather *with me* scatters" (12:30). Consequently, Jesus and his disciples form a "family" that stands apart from the rest of Israel. In relation to himself, Jesus declares that his disciples are his true relatives (12:49) and his "brothers" (28:10). In relation to one another, he asserts that they, too, are "all brothers" (23:8). In one passage, Matthew has Jesus stress at once both his uniqueness in comparison with his disciples and his "relatedness" to them: "For whoever does the will of *my Father* in heaven is *my brother, and sister, and mother*" (12:50).

Accordingly, Jesus and the disciples comprise, in Matthew's own terms, a brotherhood of the sons of God and of the disciples of Jesus. The very word "disciples" (*mathētai*) also characterizes Jesus' followers as "learners." Jesus is their "one teacher" and "Lord" (10:24; 23:8, 10), and they are his "slaves" who "learn from him" (10:24; 11:29; 13:36, 51–52). What he teaches them are the mysteries of the kingdom of heaven (13:11, 51). At times they stand in need of explanation from Jesus (13:36; 15:15) or they can be persons of "little faith" (6:30; 8:26; 14:31; 16:8). But basically, they do in fact comprehend his word (13:11, 23, 51–52; 15:15–16; 16:12; 26:2). They are not fettered with the gross ignorance that afflicts the disciples in Mark's Gospel. Indeed, Matthew has so richly endowed the disciples of his story with insight that they have simply become representative of the Christians of his own church. If, as we said earlier, Matthew has made the figure of Jesus "transparent" to his own age, he has done the same with the disciples.

We noted that in calling disciples to follow him, Jesus mediates to them the gracious, saving presence of God and his eschatological rule (5:3–11). Jesus' disciples, then, are the "salt of the earth" (5:13) and the "light of the world" (5:14). As such, they respond to their call and the teaching Jesus imparts to them by leading lives that reflect the "greater righteousness" (5:20). What this means Jesus explains in the pivotal passage 5:48: "You, therefore, shall be perfect (*teleioi*), as your heavenly Father is perfect." As this verse suggests, the disciples practice the greater righteousness when they are absolutely single-hearted, or undivided (whole, complete), in their doing of the will of God.

The ministry of the pre-Easter disciples in Matthew's Gospel is exclusively to Israel (10:6). Jesus summons the twelve and commissions them to preach the nearness of the kingdom and to heal (10:1–2, 5–8). In Matthew's scheme, this ministry of the earthly disciples is, in effect, an extension of Jesus' own earthly ministry to Israel (9:35–38).

In contradistinction to both Mark and Luke, it is within Jesus' earthly ministry that Matthew locates the founding of the "church" (16:18; 18:17).[31] The setting is his expanded version of the Marcan pericope on Peter's confession of Jesus at Caesarea Philippi (cf. 16:13–20 with Mark 8:27–30). Here Peter confesses Jesus to be the Messiah, the Son of the living God (16:16). He does so in his capacity as the first of the disciples to be called (4:18; 10:2) and therefore as their spokesman (16:15–16). As the first-called of the disciples, Peter thus becomes the foundation on which Jesus promises that he will build his church (16:18). As such, he will receive from Jesus the "keys of the kingdom of heaven," which constitute the power to decide matters that pertain to church doctrine and to church discipline (16:19). This power, however, Peter will share with the rest of the disciples (18:18).

One reason Matthew portrays Jesus as founding the church has to do with his concern to assert the unbroken continuity and legitimacy of the tradition of doctrine and practice observed by his own community. Matthew understands the earthly Son of God himself to be the source of this tradition (cf. 18:15–20; 28:20). The Son of God has entrusted it to his disciples, and they, in turn, have faithfully administered it and handed it on to the post-Easter church.

From the earthly Son who on the pages of Matthew's Gospel knows and does the Father's will, the church of Matthew learns what it is to know and do the Father's will.

Although the disciples in Matthew's Gospel comprehend the words of Jesus and know him to be the Son of God, they, like their Marcan counterparts, are unable at the last to make good on their pledge to hold to him no matter what might befall them (26:35). The upshot is that Judas betrays him (26:14-16, 47-50), the other disciples leave him and flee (26:56), and Peter denies him (26:58, 69-75). Still, upon his resurrection the Son of God sends word to the disciples through the women that they are to go to Galilee, where they will see him (28:10). In this way, he reconciles them to himself, and commissions them to their post-Easter ministry (28:16-20).

SOTERIOLOGY

There is widespread agreement among scholars that Matthew is to be seen as writing his Gospel about A.D. 90 for a Greek-speaking community of Christians which was at home in or around the city of Antioch in Syria. What was the nature of this community? What was its notion of salvation? These are the final questions we wish to explore.

The Community of Matthew[32]

Matthew writes in his version of the parable of the great supper: "The king was angry, and he sent his troops and destroyed those murderers and burned their city" (22:7). This passage suggests that Matthew's place in history is already removed from the destruction of Jerusalem by the Romans in A.D. 70. Add to this the assumption that Matthew used Mark's Gospel (A.D. 70) as one of his sources, and A.D. 90 commends itself as the probable date for the writing of his Gospel.

Matthew's community is almost certainly to be regarded as made up of persons of both Jewish and Gentile origin. Thus, there are many features of the Gospel which are uniquely suited to speak to Christians of Jewish background. The titles of majesty which Matthew ascribes to Jesus stem from Israelite and Jewish traditions. The salvation-historical prerogatives of Israel are not only acknowledged but accented ("I [Jesus] have been sent only to the lost sheep of the house of Israel" [15:24; cf. 10:6]). Although Matthew's Jesus reinterprets the Mosaic law, he nevertheless insists that he has not come to abolish it but to fulfill it (5:17). The piety of the disciples, which is described as a "righteousness" that surpasses that of the "scribes and Pharisees" (5:20), is characterized in a way that presupposes familiarity both with Jewish traditions and with contemporary Pharisaic Judaism. The Matthaean community is apparently still engaged in missionary activity among Jews (23:34).

By the same token, there are also features of the Gospel which show that Christians of Gentile background are likewise to be found among the members of Matthew's community. From the beginning to the end of his story, Matthew often casts Gentiles in a favorable light and references are made to the Christian mission to them (1:3, 5-6; 2:1-12; 8:5-13; 12:21; 13:38; 15:21-28; 24:14; 26:13; 28:18-20). In the parables of the wicked husbandmen (21:33-43) and of the great supper (22:1-10), the Matthaean Jesus already includes in his overview of the history of salvation the influx of Gentiles into the kingdom of heaven, construed as a present reality (21:41; 22:9-10).

Socioculturally, the Matthaean Christians seem to be living in an atmosphere of religious and social tension. Their mandate is to make disciples of all nations, and this appears to be provoking hostile reactions from both Jews and Gentiles. Matthew refers to the fact that Christians are being hauled into court by Gentile authorities, judicially harassed, hated "by all," and even put to death (10:18, 22; 13:21; 24:9). He tells of similar persecutions at the hands of Jews:[33] Christians are made to submit to such ill-treatment as verbal abuse (cf. 5:11), arraignment for disturbing the peace (10:17), perjured testimony in court (5:11), flogging in the local synagogues (10:17; 23:34), stoning (21:35), pursuit from city to city (10:23; 23:34), and even death (10:28; 21:35; 23:34).

Internally, the Matthaean community is an autonomous group that is materially well off. Religiously, it no longer lives under the jurisdiction of contemporary Pharisaic Judaism. In its eyes, Judaism is a "plant which my heavenly Father has not planted [and] will be rooted up" (15:13). Quite the opposite, the community of Matthew has already developed the organizational means for making its own decisions concerning matters of church doctrine and church discipline (16:19; 18:18–20). Identifiable groups within the community are such as the following: the prophets, who are itinerant missionaries who proclaim the gospel of the kingdom to Jews (10:41; 23:34) but especially to Gentiles (10:18; 24:14; 28:19); and those engaged in teaching, who are active both within the community (23:8–12) and as missionaries to the Jews (10:41; 23:34). Economically, the general way in which Matthew treats monetary matters and ethical and religious questions associated with the topic of riches is a good indication that his community is prosperous.

But this community is also rife with dissension. Under the pressure of persecution, some members are becoming apostate (13:21; 24:10). Others are betraying fellow Christians to their enemies (24:10). Still others are falling victim to the "cares of the world and the delight in riches" (13:22). There is hatred among Christians (24:10), there are false prophets who are leading others astray (7:15; 24:11), and there is such a prevalence of "wickedness" that the "love of many is growing cold" (24:12). In a situation as complex as this, what is Matthew's understanding of salvation?

The Locus of Salvation

Matthew follows Mark, we noted, in composing a kerygmatic story in which he presents Jesus as the Davidic Messiah, the royal Son of God (1:1—4:16). At the same time, Matthew does not focus his kerygmatic story so intensely on the cross per se. Instead, the central truth he proclaims is that in Jesus Messiah, his Son, God has drawn near with his end-time rule to dwell to the consummation of the age with his people, the church (1:21, 23; 18:20; 28:20). For Matthew, then, the locus of salvation is the presence of the exalted Son of God with his people.

The exalted Son of God, therefore, presides over, and resides in, his church (16:18; 18:18–20; 28:18–20). This is the place where God's end-time rule is a present reality (21:43). Through the hearing of the gospel of the kingdom (24:14; 26:13) and by submitting to baptism (28:19), people enter the sphere of God's rule. Thus summoned by Jesus Son of God through his ambassadors, these people become members of a new family (12:48–50). They become sons of God (5:45; 13:38), disciples of Jesus (10:24–25), and brothers of one another (23:8). Consequently, the Matthaean church looks upon itself as a brotherhood of the sons of God and of the disciples of Jesus.

As the Messiah Son of God, Jesus is the righteous one who knows and does his Father's will (3:13–17; 4:1–11; 11:27). Perfectly obedient to the Father, he has made final atonement for sin through his death on the cross (1:21; 26:28; 27:38–54). The forgiveness of sins he has thereby achieved, he mediates to his disciples as they celebrate their "passover meal" of bread and wine in their commemoration of him (26:26–28). Empowered by the salvation from sin he has achieved for them (1:21), they, too, become people who know and do the will of God (7:21; 12:50).

As people who know and do the will of God, the piety of the disciples of Jesus is that of the "greater righteousness" (5:20); it is the opposite of "lawlessness," of not doing the will of God (7:21–23; 13:41; 24:12). At its core, the greater righteousness is love toward God and love toward the neighbor (22:37–40). Having love toward God means being "perfect," i.e., being wholehearted in one's devotion to God (5:48). The disciple exercises such love toward God, for example, when he or she observes the law as Jesus has interpreted it (chaps. 5—7; 28:20). Having love toward the neighbor, in turn, means emulating in one's own life the self-sacrificial service Jesus has rendered to others in his life and death (20:25–28). It comes to expression above all in being forgiving toward the neighbor (6:12; 18:21–22, 35). In a community wracked by dissension such as Matthew's, this summons to forgive the neighbor possesses immediate and obvious relevance.

In the presence and under the guidance of the exalted Son of God, the Matthaean church both regulates its own affairs of doctrine and discipline (18:18–20) and carries out its mandate to make disciples of all nations (28:18–20). Although its mission is primarily to the Gentiles (28:19), it is active among Jews as well (23:34). Suffering persecution at the hands of both Jews and Gentiles, the Matthaean Christians nevertheless undertake their mission in the sure confidence that the exalted Son of God will sustain them in their task (28:20) and that the transcendent Son of man will, at the latter day, vindicate them in the sight of all the world (13:36–43; 24:29–31).

NOTES

1. On the structure of Matthew's Gospel, cf. J. D. Kingsbury, *Matthew: Structure, Christology, Kingdom* (reprint ed.; Philadelphia and London: Fortress and SPCK, 1976 and 1978), pp. 1–25.

2. On Matthew's understanding of salvation-history, cf. ibid., pp. 25–37.

3. Cf. Matt. 1:22-23; 2:5-6, 15, 17-18, 23; 4:14-16; 8:17; 12:17-21; 13:14-15, 35; 21:4-5; 27:9-10.

4. On Matthew's understanding of Jesus, cf. Kingsbury, *Matthew: Structure, Christology, Kingdom,* chaps. 2–3; idem, *Matthew* (Proclamation Commentaries; reprint ed.; Philadelphia and London: Fortress and SPCK, 1978), chap. 2. For a different view of the Matthaean Jesus, cf. J. P. Meier. *The Vision of Matthew* (Theological Inquiries; New York: Paulist, 1979).

5. On Matthew's use of the title "Son of David," cf. J. D. Kingsbury, "The Title 'Son of David' in Matthew's Gospel," *Journal of Biblical Literature,* 95 (1976), 591–602.

6. On the infancy narratives in Matthew's Gospel, cf. R. E. Brown, *The Birth of the Messiah* (Garden City: Doubleday, 1977), pp. 45–232.

7. On Matthew's use of the title "Son of Man," cf. Kingsbury, *Matthew: Structure, Christology, Kingdom,* pp. 113–22.

8. The only category of Son-of-man references which Matthew increases by any appreciable number beyond what he inherited from Mark and Q is that which pertains to the parousia (cf. 10:23; 13:41; 16:28; 19:28; 24:30; 25:31).

9. Cf. Matt. 8:19–20; 9:3 and 6; 11:7 and 16 and 19; 12:2 and 8, 24 and 32, 38 and 40; also 26:59 and 64.

10. Cf. Matt. 17:9 and 12, 22–23; 20:18–19; 26:2, 24–25, 45; also 12:40.

11. Cf. Matt. 10:23; 13:40–43; 16:27–28; 19:28; 24:27, 30, 37, 39, 44; 25:31; 26:64.

12. This point is made especially well by B. Gerhardsson, "Gottes Sohn als Diener Gottes," *Studia Theologica,* 27 (1973), 73–106.

13. Cf. Mark 8:38; 11:25; 13:32; 14:36.

14. Cf. J. Schneider, *"Proserchomai,"* Theological Dictionary of the New Testament, II (1964), 683.

15. Cf., e.g., Matt. 2:2, 11; 9:18; 14:33; 28:9, 17.

16. Cf., e.g., Mark 5:9, 30; 6:38; 8:23; 9:12, 16, 21, 33; 10:3; 14:14.

17. Cf. Mark 1:45; 6:48; 7:24; 9:30; Mark 6:5 with Matt. 13:58; Mark 11:13 with Matt. 21:19.

18. Cf., e.g., Matt. 12:38; 19:16; 22:16, 24, 36; 26:25, 49.

19. Cf., e.g., Matt. 8:2, 6, 8, 21, 25; 14:28, 30.

20. On Matthew's use of the title "Lord," cf. Kingsbury, *Matthew: Structure, Christology, Kingdom,* pp. 103–13.

21. Cf. Matt. 3:13—4:11; 8:23—9:1; 15:21–28; 16:13–20; also 17:22.

22. On chap. 13, the "parable chapter" of Matthew's Gospel, cf. J. D. Kingsbury, *The Parables of Jesus in Matthew 13* (reprint ed.; London and St. Louis: SPCK and Clayton Publishing House, 1977).

23. Cf., e.g., Matt. 8:25 with Mark 4:38; Matt. 17:4 with Mark 9:5; Matt. 17:15 with Mark 9:17.

24. On "new-Moses typology" in Matthew's Gospel, cf. Kingsbury, *Matthew: Structure, Christology, Kingdom,* pp. 89–92.

25. On the antitheses of the Sermon on the Mount, cf. J. P. Meier, *Law and History in Matthew's Gospel* (AnBib 71; Rome: Biblical Institute Press, 1976), chap. 4.

26. On Matt. 23, cf. D. E. Garland, *The Intention of Matthew 23* (NovTSup 52; Leiden: E. J. Brill, 1979).

27. On the healing ministry of Jesus, cf. B. Gerhardsson, *The Mighty Acts of Jesus according to Matthew* (*Scripta Minora* 5; Lund: CWK Gleerup, 1979).

28. Cf. Matt. 4:23, 24; 8:7, 16; 9:35; [12:10]; 12:15, 22; 14:14; 15:30; 17:18; 19:2; 21:14.

29. Cf. Matt. 4:23; 8:16–17; 9:35; 11:5; 12:15; 14:14; 15:30; 19:2.

30. On Matthew's treatment of the passion of Jesus, cf. B. Gerhardsson, "Jésus livré et abandonné," *Revue Biblique,* 76 (1969), 206-27; D. P. Senior, *The Passion Narrative according to Matthew* (BETL 39; Gembloux: J. Duculot, 1975).

31. On the organizational structure of Matthew's church, cf. J. D. Kingsbury, "The Figure of Peter in Matthew's Gospel as a Theological Problem," *Journal of Biblical Literature,* 98 (1979), 67–83.

32. On the community of Matthew, cf. Kingsbury, *Matthew* (Proclamation Commentaries), chap. 4; idem, "The Verb *Akolouthein* ('to follow') as an Index of Matthew's View of His Community," *Journal of Biblical Literature,* 97 (1978), 56–73.

33. On the theme of Jewish persecution in Matthew's Gospel, cf. D. R. A. Hare, *The Theme of Jewish Persecution of Christians in the Gospel according to St. Matthew* (SNTSMS 6; Cambridge: Cambridge University, 1967).

CHAPTER FOUR

LUKE

We have seen thus far that the focus in Q is on the parousia of Jesus, that in Mark's Gospel it is on his cross, and that in Matthew's Gospel it is on his abiding presence with his people, the church. In the Gospel according to Luke, the focus is different still. Simply put, it is on the salvation that God in Jesus proffers to Israel.

THE ACCOMPLISHMENT OF LUKE

Luke alone of the synoptic evangelists follows the literary convention of his day and introduces his Gospel with a prologue (1:1-4). In this prologue, he informs the reader of the nature and purpose of his Gospel.

Luke states in the prologue that, by his time, "many" have already undertaken to write a "narrative" concerning the "things which have been fulfilled among us" (1:1). Of immediate interest here is the reference Luke makes to existing documents he has had at his disposal in the writing of his Gospel. In terms of the two-source hypothesis, these documents can be identified as Q, Mark, and sources peculiar to Luke himself.

Noteworthy is the way in which Luke has arranged these materials. The infancy and resurrection stories (chaps. 1—2; 24) bracket the Gospel and stem on the whole from Luke's special sources. The sayings of Q appear in two sections in particular, in 6:20—7:35 and in 9:51—18:14. By contrast, it is from Mark that Luke derives the general outline of his Gospel (3:1—6:19; 8:4—9:50; 18:15—24:11). Moreover, because the shape of this outline is such that it reaches its culmination in the accounts of the suffering and exaltation of Jesus, it is obvious that Luke's Gospel, like the Gospels of Mark and Matthew, stands in the tradition of the "passion kerygma" of the early church (cf. 1 Cor. 15:3-5).

As for the nature of his Gospel, Luke himself designates it as a "narrative" (1:1). This narrative begins with the births of John the Baptist and of Jesus and concludes with the death, resurrection, and ascension of Jesus. Luke maintains that this narrative is both "accurate" and "orderly" because he has subjected the matters of which he writes to careful scrutiny (1:3). Does this mean, then, that Luke's Gospel is what the Gospels of Mark and Matthew are not, namely, a biography, or literary documentary, of the life of Jesus?

The answer is negative. Through his use of the verb "to narrate" (*diēgeisthai*), Luke indicates how the noun "narrative" (*diēgēsis*) is to be understood. Thus, in 8:39 Luke employs the verb "to proclaim" (*kēryssein*) as the virtual equivalent of the verb "to narrate" (RSV: "declare"). But if in Luke's mind "to proclaim" is indeed the virtual equivalent of "to narrate," we see that Luke regards the "narrative" he has authored as "proclamatory," or "kerygmatic," in nature. On balance, therefore, Luke's Gospel is not different in kind from that of either Mark or Matthew: it is of the nature of a "kerygmatic story."

But should Luke's narrative be kerygmatic and not biographical in nature, in what sense can it also be said to be "accurate" and "orderly"? Not in the sense that it is to be thought of as more reliable, factually or chronologically, than, say, the Gospel of Mark. Luke himself rules this notion out, for he admits to the use of traditions and sources, one of which appears to have been Mark itself. What Luke is claiming is that his narrative places God's action in Jesus Messiah in proper perspective for the people for whom he has written it. In so doing, it enables Theophilus, for example, to discern the true meaning of what God has accomplished in Jesus.

This raises the question of the purpose for which Luke has written his narrative. The addressee he names is "Theophilus," a Roman official perhaps (1:3). But Luke likewise makes reference in the first two verses of his prologue to "us," i.e., to persons who are post-ascension Christians. In 1:2, the pronoun "us" denotes Luke himself and his own community. Hence, Luke does in fact aim his narrative at Theophilus, but also at the Christians of his church. And with what goal in mind? As Luke himself defines it: ". . . in order that you might know the certainty (truth) concerning the things about which you have been informed (instructed)" (1:4).

Accordingly, Luke composes his kerygmatic narrative to the end that it might communicate certainty and truth. For the Christians of his community, this means that they will be confirmed in the faith they already hold. For Theophilus, who may not have been a Christian, this means that he will be challenged by the claim that the Christian message always makes upon those who hear it (24:47; Acts 2:36–39).

The larger issue we are pursuing is the accomplishment of Luke. We have observed that Luke has created from his sources a kerygmatic story the purpose of which is to communicate certainty and truth concerning God's action in Jesus Messiah. With this in mind, we want to examine Luke's story further.

Luke's Gospel as a Kerygmatic Story

Luke's kerygmatic story about Jesus is broader in scope than even Matthew's. Whereas Matthew's story runs from the birth of Jesus to his resurrection, Luke's story begins with the annunciation of the birth of John the Baptist (1:5–25) and closes with the pericope on the ascension of Jesus (24:50–53).

In comparison with the first two Gospels, the topical outline Luke follows in narrating his story is distinctive in its own right. Luke prefaces his story, as we noted, with a prologue (1:1–4). In the first larger section of the story itself, he introduces the reader to John the Baptist, the unique prophet of God, and to Jesus, the Messiah and Son of God (1:5—4:13). Next, Luke tells of the public ministry of Jesus. While Jesus' ministry is to all Israel,[1] he initially wanders for the most part in Galilee (4:14—9:50). Then he embarks on a long journey to Jerusalem (9:51—19:44). This journey unfolds in five stages, and each stage is marked by the recurrent notation that he is going toward Jerusalem (9:51; 13:22; 17:11; 18:31; 19:28). Once in Jerusalem, Jesus discharges a ministry of teaching in the temple (19:45—21:38). And this, in turn, is followed by the events that surround his passion, crucifixion, resurrection, and ascension (22:1—24:53).

A glance at this topical outline reveals that, at the hands of Luke, the story of the life and ministry of Jesus has largely become a story of Jesus' journey to Jerusalem.[2] The reason the story of Jesus assumes this shape has to do with Luke's notion of the history of salvation. We shall consider this in detail shortly. Suffice it to say that Luke views the life and ministry of Jesus as the fulfillment of God's long-prophesied purpose to grant Israel salvation in the last times (1:31–33, 68–75; 2:10–11, 30–32). Thus, as Jesus moves through Galilee and toward Jerusalem, he is carrying out this divine purpose. Moreover, Jerusalem, and with it the temple, is the center of Israel (2:22, 38, 41; 4:9; 13:33). Hence, by casting the ministry of Jesus in the form of a journey to Jerusalem, Luke deftly directs attention to the theme of his Gospel: in Jesus Messiah, God proffers salvation to Israel.

The Theological Claim of Luke's Gospel

To enable the reader (e.g., Theophilus) to perceive the story of Jesus aright, Luke places it in context. On the one hand, this context is as broad as history itself, for it stretches from creation to consummation. Luke indicates this by tracing the genealogy of Jesus to Adam and to God in the one instance (3:38) and, in the other, by describing the coming of Jesus Son of man at the end of all things (21:25–27). He also points to this broad context by relating the story of Jesus to world history (2:1–3; 3:1).

On the other hand, the context Luke more often has in view is that of the history of salvation, the history of God's dealings with his people. In this regard, Luke distinguishes between the "time of Israel" (1:54–55, 68), which is the "time of prophecy" (1:70; 24: 25–27, 44–45), and the "time of fulfillment" (1:1; 24:44).[3] For its part, the time of fulfillment is better construed in Lucan thought as the "time of salvation" (2:30–32). This is because the marks of this time are the presence of the Savior, Jesus (1:69; 2:11), of the Holy Spirit (1:41, 67; 2:25; 3:22), and of God's eschatological kingdom (17:21). This time of salvation, in turn, encompasses the ministries to Israel of Jesus (4:18–19), of the twelve (9:1–2), and of the seventy (10:1) and the ministry to both Israel and the Gentiles of the church (24:47–48; cf. Acts 1:8). Indeed, the time of salvation will have run its course only with the appearance of the heavenly Son of man at the end of time (21:27).

Although Luke's notion of the time of salvation is expansive, covering a whole succession of ministries, he nevertheless leaves no doubt that it is in Jesus that the whole of this time has its center.

There is but one Savior, whether of Israel or of the Gentiles (2:11, 30–32), and it is to him that the several ministries comprising the time of salvation attest. As Luke has Peter declare in Acts: ". . . there is salvation in no one else, for there is no other name under heaven given among men by which we must be saved" (4:12).

We have made no mention so far of John the Baptist. How does he figure in Luke's scheme of the history of salvation? On this score, Luke's treatment of John is like that of Q: John stands on the threshold between the old and the new. Thus, John is a "prophet" (1:76; 7:26) and consequently belongs to the "time of prophecy" (16:16). However, he is also "more than a prophet" (7:26): he is God's end-time "messenger" sent to proclaim in Israel a baptism of repentance so as to "make ready for the Lord [God] a people prepared" (1:16–17; 3:3; 7:27). When seen in this light, John fits easily into the "time of salvation." Consequently, Luke's picture of John is that of one in whom the two epochs of prophecy and of salvation meet: John closes out the one by paving the way for the other.

This brings us to the dual question of the accomplishment of Luke and of the theological claim of his Gospel. Structurally, Luke has created from his sources a kerygmatic story in which he describes the life and ministry of Jesus under the form of a journey from Galilee to Jerusalem, the center of Israel. The context into which Luke places this story is the history of salvation. Here the time of prophecy gives way to the time of fulfillment and of salvation. The story of Jesus, of course, is foundational to the latter, the time of salvation. Luke's accomplishment, therefore, is that he has fashioned a kerygmatic story against the backdrop of the history of salvation whereby he portrays Jesus as proffering salvation to Israel. The theological claim this story advances is that Jesus is in truth the Savior of Israel. Since Luke's Gospel contains within it the seeds of the Book of Acts, it advances the claim as well that Jesus is also the Savior of the Gentiles (2:30–32; 24:47).

THE FIGURE OF JESUS

Christology throughout the NT is intimately related to theology, to the knowledge of God. Comparatively, Luke has more to say about Jesus' relationship to God than do Mark, Matthew, or the redactors of Q.

Take, for example, the name "Jesus." It means "God is salvation," and harbors within it the confessional truth that God is at work in Jesus. To give pointed expression to this truth, Luke does something these other writers do not do, namely, he calls Jesus "Savior."

In designating Jesus as "Savior," Luke is taking a term of majesty for God and attributing it to Jesus. In OT and Jewish thought, God is the one Savior of his people (Isa. 45:21) who delivers them from bondage, whether it be from that of foreign domination or of evil.[4] Thus, the psalmist in Habakkuk cries out: "I shall rejoice in God my Savior!" (3:18 LXX). Significantly, this selfsame passage is echoed by Mary in the Magnificat: ". . . my spirit exults in God my Savior" (Luke 1:47). But if in the Magnificat it is God who is praised as Savior, in the announcement of the angel to the shepherds it is Jesus who is called Savior: ". . . for to you is born this day in the city of David a Savior . . ." (2:11). And with what objective in mind does Luke transfer the title of Savior to Jesus? He does so in order to affirm that God has determined to make available in Jesus the deliverance, or salvation, that otherwise only he can accomplish. Then, too, this salvation, as we shall observe, is that which attends the presence of God's end-time kingdom in Jesus and the forgiveness of sins.

Another divine title that Luke appropriates for Jesus is that of "Lord." Although Jesus is also referred to as Lord in Q, Mark, and Matthew, in these documents it has not yet become the "full-blown" title that Luke makes of it. "Lord" (*kyrios*) is the translation for "Jahweh" found in the Greek OT (LXX). As the Lord, God rules over the whole world; the psalmist exclaims: "Shout to God with loud songs of joy! For the Lord, the Most High, is terrible, a great king over all the earth" (Ps. 47:1–2). For his part, Luke gives reverence to God in the words of Jesus as the "Lord of heaven and earth" (10:21).

Luke does with "Lord" what he has done with "Savior," namely, applies it to Jesus. At 2:11, the angel says to the shepherds: ". . . for to you is born this day in the city of David a Savior, who is Christ the Lord!" Because Acts 2:36 ostensibly suggests that Jesus does not become Lord until his resurrection, it is necessary to stress that, on the contrary, Luke regards him as being Lord from birth (cf. also 1:43). What Luke has in mind in giving Jesus the title of Lord is succinctly stated in the passage 1:31–33: ". . . you

[Mary] shall call his name Jesus . . . and the Lord God will give to him the throne of his father David, and he will reign over the house of Jacob for ever. . . ." In other words, Jesus is Lord because he is the one through whom God, the Lord, chooses to exercise his rule over Israel and, we might add, over the Gentiles as well. And finally, because Jesus is in fact the one through whom the Lord God exercises his divine rule, Luke will refer to him either as the "Lord Jesus" (24:3; cf. Acts) or as "the Lord" (cf., e.g., 7:13, 19; 10:1, 39, 41). These latter terms underline the divine authority with which Jesus acts.

Jesus as the Messiah, the Son of God and the Servant of God

"Savior" and "Lord" are titles of majesty which are indicative of God as King. Applied to Jesus, they characterize him as the one through whom God acts. Throughout his story, Luke portrays Jesus as the Messiah—King (cf. 23:2). In so doing, he continues in the tradition of Mark.

Luke employs the first major section of his story to introduce the reader to John the Baptist and Jesus and to describe the unique role that is theirs in the history of salvation (1:5—4:13). In the pericope on the annunciation of the birth of Jesus (1:26–38), Luke projects, perhaps better than anywhere else in his Gospel, his broad understanding of the person of Jesus.[5] Of special importance are these words which Gabriel speaks to Mary: "And behold, you will conceive in your womb and bear a son, and you shall call his name Jesus; he will be great and will be called the Son of the Most High; and the Lord God will give to him the throne of his father David, and he will reign over the house of Jacob for ever; and of his kingdom there will be no end" (1:31–33). Add to this description of Jesus Luke's further view that the Son of God is at the same time the Servant of God (2:43, 49; Acts 3:13, 26; 4:27, 30), and the following sketch of the Lucan Jesus emerges: Jesus, the Messiah—King from the line of David, is the Son of God and the Servant of God.

Luke makes more of the title "Messiah," or "Christ" ("Anointed One"), than do Mark and Matthew. It is a comprehensive term that marks Jesus as the final, supreme agent of God in the history of salvation (2:26; 9:20). Jesus Messiah is King (23:2) and Davidid (2:11; 20:41–44). He comes in fulfillment of prophecy and hence inaugurates the eschatological time of salvation (7:18–23). Indeed, his birth (2:10–11), suffering (24:26, 46), resurrection (24:46), ascension (24:26), and parousia (Acts 3:20) encompass this time. In him, God remembers his promises and grants to Israel the "consolation" it has long awaited (2:25–26; Isa. 40:1; 49:13). His coming, therefore, is cause for "great joy" (2:10–11) and "praise" to God (2:11, 13).

Luke is eager that Jesus should be known and confessed to be God's Messiah. Throughout the Galilean phase of Jesus' ministry (4:14—9:50), Luke punctuates his story with questions and answers that concern the identity of Jesus.[6] He does so in order that Jesus might at the last elicit from Peter, on behalf of the disciples, a climactic declaration as to who Jesus is.

Thus, at 5:21 the scribes and the Pharisees, taking offense at Jesus, begin to question one another, "Who is this that speaks blasphemies? Who can forgive sins but God only?"[7] At 7:49, the guests at table with Jesus similarly ask themselves, "Who is this, who even forgives sins?" At 8:25, the disciples, in fear and astonishment, query one another, "Who then is this, that he commands even wind and water, and they obey him?" At 9:7–9, a perplexed Herod, having heard rumors to the effect that Jesus is John raised from the dead, or Elijah redivivus, or one of the old prophets come back to life, wonders aloud, ". . . who is this about whom I hear such things?" Then, at 9:18 Jesus himself seizes the initiative and asks the disciples, "Who do the crowds say that I am?" When the disciples respond by repeating the same rumors Herod has heard (9: 19), Jesus presses them with the question, "But who do you say that I am?" (9:20). To this Peter replies, "The Christ of God!" (9:20; cf. 2:26). This answer of Peter is not, of course, Luke's final word on the identity of Jesus per se. As we shall see, it must be supplemented by God's word at the transfiguration (9:35) and augmented by the story of the passion (24:25–27, 45–47). Nevertheless, Peter's reply does constitute a true perception of Jesus and underlines the fundamental importance in Luke's Gospel of the title Messiah.

Because he is a royal figure, Jesus Messiah can also be called

"King (of the Jews)" (19:38; 23:2, 3, 37, 38). Still, this title, in a document to Theophilus, for example, has great potential for being misconstrued. After all, the inscription which is affixed to the cross of Jesus in the crucifixion-scene and which cites the charge for which he dies reads: "This is the King of the Jews" (23:38). Within his story, therefore, Luke sets forth the correct meaning of the title King against the background of its misinterpretation.

Those who falsify the term King by loading it with seditious connotations are the leaders of the Jews. Before Pilate, the Jewish leaders level this accusation against Jesus: "We have found this man perverting our nation, and forbidding us to give tribute to Caesar, and saying that he himself is Messiah, a king" (23:2). Luke, of course, depicts Pilate as investigating this accusation and even as sending Jesus to Herod for interrogation (23:3–12). But after Jesus has been returned to him, Pilate has only this report to issue to the Jews: ". . . I have found this man guilty of none of your accusations against him; neither has Herod" (23:14–15).

But if Luke shows that it is wrong to interpret "King" to mean that Jesus is out to establish a Jewish state, what does King mean? Luke answers this question in the same context in which the title is subject to misunderstanding. In the pericope on the crucifixion of Jesus, Luke sketches a scene in which Jesus, himself at the point of death, sovereignly grants to the repentant criminal admittance to the kingdom of God (23:42–43). In Luke's eyes, then, Jesus is in fact the King, for despite his condemnation to death, entrance into the sphere of God's end-time kingdom is only through him (cf. 19:38).

In telling of Jesus Messiah, Luke is by no means neglectful of his Davidic pedigree. Even so, "Son of David" does not become the prominent christological strain in his Gospel that it does in Matthew's. According to Luke, it is through Joseph, who is of the "house and lineage of David" (2:4; cf. 1:27), that Jesus becomes both the "son of Joseph" (4:22) and a Davidid, a descendant of David (3:23, 31). Indeed, Jesus is even born in Bethlehem, the "city of David," owing to the fact that Joseph, with Mary, travels there in compliance with Caesar's decree for a "worldwide" census (2:1–4, 11).

But Luke's interest in Jesus as the Son of David is not, finally, biographical in nature. It is grounded instead in his conception of the fulfillment of prophecy. Specifically, Luke holds that, in Jesus, God makes good on his age-old promise to David: ". . . I will raise up your son after you . . . and I will establish the throne of his kingdom for ever" (cf. 1:32–33 to 2 Sam. 7:12–13). Still, although Luke retreats not an inch from his affirmation that Jesus Messiah is the Son of David, the latter is not without its problematic. As we saw above, Luke is sensitive to the fact that Jesus must die as the King of the Jews charged with having tried to subvert the power of Rome (23:2–5, 24, 37). Hence, even as Luke insists that Jesus is in truth the Son of David, he takes pains to show in what manner it is that he wields his "Davidic authority." It is not to foment revolution, but to carry out an important aspect of the messianic ministry entrusted to him. In the programmatic statement Jesus makes in the synagogue at Nazareth, he announces that he has been sent "to proclaim . . . recovery of sight to the blind" (4:18). It is in line with this messianic mandate, therefore, that Jesus, in his capacity as the Son of David, saves through healing the Jericho-beggar whose blindness has heretofore alienated him from the community of Israel (18:35–43).

Luke's broad understanding of Jesus in his Gospel, we said, is that he is the Messiah—King from the line of David, the Son of God and the Servant of God. Thus far, we have discussed Luke's description of Jesus as the Messiah, the King of the Jews and the Son of David. However, the most important title Luke predicates to Jesus, along with "Messiah," is that of the "Son of God." In fact, at times it appears that the titles "Messiah" and "Son of God" approximate each other so closely in Luke's Gospel that they virtually become synonymous (cf. 1:35 to 2:11; 4:41; 22:67 to 22:70). Yet on the whole, Luke seems to employ "Son of God" to elucidate the underlying intention of "Messiah." In this respect, he proceeds much as Mark and Matthew do also.

Luke makes it clear from the outset of his story that Jesus Messiah is "more" than merely the scion of David. In the key pericopes on the annunciation of Jesus' birth, the genealogy, and the question about David's Son, Luke defines this "more" in terms of Jesus' also being the Son of God.

Thus, in the story of the annunciation Luke shows that the child Jesus, miraculously conceived in the virgin Mary by the power of God's Holy Spirit, has his origin in God and is therefore the Son of God (1:27, 32, 35). In the genealogy, Luke calls attention to Jesus' divine sonship in double fashion. For one thing, when he names Jesus the son of Joseph, he qualifies the entry so as to allude to the conception of the Son of God by the Spirit of God: "Jesus," Luke writes, "the son, *as it was supposed, of Joseph*" (3:23). For another thing, Luke arranges the names of the genealogy in an ascending order so that the emphasis falls on the last link in the chain: "Jesus . . . the son of Joseph . . . the son of David . . . the son of God" (3:23, 31, 38). And in the passage on the question about David's Son, Luke has Jesus himself affirm that the Messiah, who is indeed the Son of David, is at the same time "more" than this, namely, the Son of God and the Lord (cf. 20:41–44 to 1:32–33, 35; 2:11; Acts 2:33–36).

But more exactly, what does it mean for Luke to designate Jesus as the Son of God? Primarily, Luke utilizes this title to focus on the unique relationship that exists between God the Father and Jesus, the royal Messiah. This unique relationship begins already with the conception of Jesus: he is conceived miraculously as the Holy Spirit "comes upon" the virgin Mary and "overshadows" her (1:27, 35). Moreover, Jesus Son of God is one who is "holy" (1:35), i.e., "set apart" for special service to God. He is also "great" (1:32), after the fashion of kings and especially God, the ruler over all the earth (Ps. 47:2). It is to Jesus Son of God, therefore, that God grants dominion (1:32–33), and it is in him that God's eschatological kingdom becomes a present reality (1:33; 11:20; 17:21).

Other facets of the unique relationship that exists between God and the Son of God are also highlighted by Luke. In preparation for his messianic ministry, Jesus Son of God submits to baptism and to temptation. At his baptism, he is both empowered and attested to by God: empowered by God with his Holy Spirit and attested to by God as being his only, or unique, Son whom he has chosen for messianic ministry (3:22; cf. 9:35). In the temptation, two matters are stressed. The one is that the messianic ministry for which God has chosen Jesus is of cosmic significance: Jesus Son of God must contend with the devil, who is himself a ruler and lays claim to the world as his kingdom (4:1–2, 6; 11:14–22; Acts 10:38). The second matter is that it is precisely in withstanding the three "tests" of the devil that Jesus reveals what the essential ingredient of divine sonship is: absolute obedience to the will of his Father (4:1–13).

The absolute obedience that Jesus Son of God renders to God points to his oneness with God. Luke gives expression to the latter in these words of Jesus: "All things have been delivered to me by my Father; and no one knows who the Son is except the Father, or who the Father is except the Son and any one to whom the Son chooses to reveal him" (10:22). If these words are interpreted in terms of what has been said above, they can serve as the basis for a summary statement on Luke's understanding of Jesus as the Son of God. This summary statement is the following: Jesus is the Son of God, for, conceived by the Holy Spirit and chosen and empowered by God for messianic ministry, he knows God completely, obeys him perfectly, and acts on his divine authority to reveal him to those who become his disciples; as the one who is thus the bearer of God's kingdom, he overthrows the kingdom of Satan and, as Savior, Messiah, and Lord, restores Israel (cf. 2:11 to 1:32–33).

It remains to point out that Luke also identifies Jesus Son of God as the "Servant" of God (2:43; cf. Acts 4:27, 30 to 13:33). The Greek term *pais* facilitates this identification, because it can denote either "son" (or "boy") or "servant." In the pericope on the twelve-year-old Jesus in the temple, for example, the "boy Jesus" (2:43), who is the "son" of Mary and Joseph (2:48), is at the same time the "Son" of God (2:49). Moreover, when the boy Jesus puts the rhetorical question to his parents, "Did you not know that it is necessary for me to be about the things of my Father?" (2:49), Luke intends for these words to allude to the salvation-historical mission that Jesus Son of God is destined to carry out (1:32–33, 68–75; 2:30–32, 34). To Luke's way of thinking, however, the title Son of God as such tends to lay stress on the personal relationship that exists between God and Jesus. By contrast, the title Servant commends itself when the mission of Jesus is in some sense in view. This is the case in this story of the twelve-year-old Jesus and also in the passages in Acts in which this title occurs (Acts 3:13, 26; 4:27,

30). Later, in the programmatic narrative on Jesus' rejection in Nazareth, we shall once again have occasion to see Jesus Son of God in his role as the Servant of God.

Jesus as the Son of Man

Like Matthew, Luke, too, has appropriated Son-of-man references from both Mark and Q. Like Matthew, Luke has also followed Mark's lead and applied the title Son of man to the three main phases of Jesus' ministry: to his "earthly (present) activity," to his "suffering," and to his "future coming." At the same time, Luke does not simply bind himself to Mark's use of this title. He adapts it to meet his own concerns, and he has likewise made some few additions to the traditional fund of Son-of-man references.[8]

We recall that in neither Mark nor in Matthew is Son of man what may be termed a "confessional" title. That is to say, Jesus is not "confessed" in them to be the Son of man the way the disciples in Matthew (14:33; 16:16) and the centurion in Mark (15:39) confess him to be the Son of God. On the contrary, Son of man is, we said, better described as a "public" title. In what sense? In the sense that it is the designation by which Jesus refers to himself as he interacts in public with (the crowds and) his opponents, tells his disciples what his opponents and Gentiles are about to do to him, and depicts himself at his parousia as being vindicated in the sight of all the world.

By and large, Luke's use of the title Son of man is not dissimilar to this. Thus, for Luke, too, Son of man is not a "confessional" title. Never is Jesus confessed in his story, or even addressed, as the Son of man. No, when it comes to the question of Jesus' identity in Luke's story (5:21; 7:49; 8:25; 9:9, 18, 20), the decisive answer that is given is not that Jesus is the Son of man but that he is "the Messiah of God" (9:20).

To be sure, this answer, uttered by Peter, begs to be supplemented in at least two respects. First, Luke shows that God himself has his own answer to the question, "Who is this?" God makes this known to the three disciples on the mount of the transfiguration: "This is my Son, my Chosen" (9:35; cf. 3:22). In Luke's eyes, then, essential to being the Messiah of God is being the Son of God.

Second, Peter's answer also begs to be supplemented because the full implications of what it means for Jesus to be the Messiah of God cannot be known until after the events of the passion have taken place. This explains why Jesus responds to Peter's confession by commanding the disciples to "tell this to no one" (9:21; cf. 9:36). It also explains why the disciples in Luke's story are not permitted to understand the passion predictions Jesus makes (9:45; 18:34).[9] In any event, the grand result of the fact that Luke keeps intact from 9:21 until the end of his Gospel the command of Jesus to "tell no one" is that he thereby shows that it is only against the backdrop of the rest of his story that one can understand aright what it means for Peter to confess Jesus to be "the Messiah of God" (9:20). Specifically, what one must add to Peter's confession to understand it aright is the divinely revealed knowledge that the Messiah of God is the one whom God has ordained to suffer, to rise, and to ascend to glory (24:45–46; cf. 24:25–27).

Properly construed, therefore, "the Messiah of God" is the central confessional title of Luke's Gospel. It is so because to acknowledge Jesus to be the Messiah is to perceive him to be the royal Son of God, the bearer of God's eschatological kingdom, and the one whom God has chosen from of old to suffer and to rise so that salvation might be preached in his name (1:32–33, 35; 24:25–27, 46–47). In short, to acknowledge Jesus to be the "Messiah" is to have been given, by the gift of divine revelation, insight into the mystery of the person and mission of Jesus (10:21–22).

To this, one more thing must be added. If it is correct to say that "the Messiah of God" is the central confessional title of Luke's Gospel, it is nevertheless also true that this title is frequently conjoined in Acts with "Lord." In fact, in key passages in both the Gospel and Acts Luke employs both of these titles to answer the question about Jesus, "Who is this?" In 2:11, the angel announces to the shepherds, ". . . for to you is born today a Savior, who is Messiah Lord." And in Acts 2:36, Peter proclaims to the Jews on Pentecost, "Let all the house of Israel therefore know assuredly that God has made him [Jesus] both Lord and Messiah. . . ." Luke ascribes many titles to Jesus. Chief among these, however, are "Messiah" and "Lord."

We turn now to the title Son of man. It functions quite differently in Luke's Gospel from Messiah, as is easily demonstrated. As we saw, the title Messiah is the climactic answer to an entire series of questions aimed at eliciting from Peter, within the circle of the disciples, a true estimate of the identity of Jesus (9:18–21). By contrast, Son of man occurs only on the lips of Jesus, and no aura of secrecy surrounds it. On the contrary, as early as 5:24 Jesus refers to himself as the Son of man in the audience both of the Jewish "crowd" and of "Pharisees and teachers of the law" who have come from "every village of Galilee and Judea and from Jerusalem" (5:17, 19, 26). In other words, the Lucan Jesus designates himself as the Son of man before the whole of Israel. What is more, at 6:5; 7:34; 9:58; and 11:30 the same phenomenon occurs: in the presence of "some of the Pharisees" (6:2) or of the "men of this generation" (7:31), or of a "certain man" (9:57), or of the "crowds" (11:29), Jesus again makes reference to himself as the Son of man. And at 19:10, Luke describes yet another such scene, but one that is peculiar to his Gospel: in the sight of the "grumbling crowd" (19:3, 7) Jesus exclaims, "For the Son of man has come to seek and to save the lost."

What these examples reveal is that Luke utilizes Son of man, as do Mark and Matthew as well, as a "public" title. Namely, Son of man is the title Jesus ascribes to himself as he interacts in public with a stranger or the Jewish crowds or their leaders, who are his implacable opponents. In a comparable vein, Son of man is also the title that the Lucan Jesus uses when he tells his disciples, as in the passion predictions, what he is about to endure at the hands of his opponents and Judas: he is about to be betrayed into the hands of sinful men and Gentiles,[10] be rejected, mistreated, and made to suffer,[11] be killed (9:22; 18:33; 24:7), but then also be raised (9:22; 18:33; 24:7).

There is one passage in which Luke, probably in dependence upon Q, extends the sufferings of the Son of man to the disciples. In the passion prediction of 18:32–33, it is said of Jesus Son of man that he will be mocked, shamefully treated, spit upon, and scourged. Analogously, Jesus says to the disciples in one of his beatitudes: "Blessed are you when men hate you, exclude you, revile you, and cast out your name as evil *on account of the Son of man*" (6:22). The idea is patent: Jesus, as the suffering Son of man, becomes a model for the disciples; the kind of suffering the "world" inflicts on him it will also inflict on the disciples.

Finally, Luke affirms that Jesus, who has publicly presented himself in Israel as the Son of man and been made to suffer at the hands of Jews and Gentiles, will also be vindicated before the world as the Son of man. Still, Luke conceives of this vindication in a somewhat different manner from Mark and Matthew. As Luke envisages it, the vindication of Jesus Son of man will occur in two stages. The first stage is the ascension, at which time the "Son of man shall be seated at the right hand of the power of God" (22:69). And the second stage, which will confirm the reality of the first one, is the parousia, at which time all the world shall "see the Son of man coming in a cloud with power and great glory" (21:27). Compared with Matthew, Luke places a low premium on depicting the parousia as an apocalyptic panorama of the last judgment (cf., e.g., Matt. 25:31–46). Instead, he employs parousia passages to exhort his community to perseverence, faithfulness, and preparedness in the face of temptations and persecution (12:40; 17:22; 18:8; 21:36). Given the situation of his community, Luke stresses that not only will Jesus Son of man stand vindicated at the last before the world, but so will the Christian disciples who have suffered in following his example (21:27–28).

How does the "public" title of Son of man relate to the "confessional" title of Messiah in Luke's Gospel? For Luke, "Messiah" identifies Jesus as the long-prophesied Davidic King who is the Son and Servant of God. In the course of his ministry, Jesus leads Peter, on behalf of the disciples, to confess him to be the Messiah (9:20). Of course such supernatural beings as God (3:22), the devil (4:1–13), and demons (4:41) also know that he is the Messiah Son of God. But Israel as such does not know this and, in fact, repudiates the inference (4:16–30; 22:66–71). In Israel, Jesus publicly refers to himself, before the crowds and his opponents, as the "Son of man" (cf., e.g., 5:24; 6:5; 7:34). Moreover, he also predicts the suffering that the "world," i.e., his Jewish and Gentile opponents, will inflict upon him, the Son of man (cf., e.g., 18:32–33). But he likewise predicts that, following his suffering, God will also vindicate him as the Son of man. This will occur, first, in his resurrection and ascension (22:69) and, second, in the sight of all the world when he comes in power and glory (21:27). What is more, his vindication in the sight of all the world will also be the vindication of the disciples (21:27–28), for the "world" will subject them to suffering in the same way as it does him (6:22).

If, then, Luke works in his Gospel with Messiah as a "confessional" title and with Son of man as a "public" title, is there some juncture at which he brings the two lines together? Mark and Matthew do so, we remember, at the point of the parousia. For his part, Luke does so at the point of the ascension. In 22:66–71, the Son of man who is seated at the right hand of the power of God is identified as the Messiah Son of God. Accordingly, even as the risen and exalted Son of man, Jesus remains the Messiah, the Son of God.

THE MISSION OF JESUS

Luke begins his story of Jesus by speaking first of John the Baptist. While Luke paints John in some of the same colors as Mark and Matthew, his portrait of John is by no means a reproduction of theirs. Thus, Mark and Matthew both describe John as Elijah redivivus, the forerunner specifically of Jesus (Mark 9:11–13; Matt. 17:10–13). Luke, on the other hand, presents John more generally as the forerunner of the "time of salvation" (1:77; 3:6). To be sure, Jesus is for Luke the indispensable figure in the time of salvation. For this reason, he pictures John as temporally preceding Jesus (3:15–16; Acts 13:23–25). But Luke is just as quick to depict John as the forerunner of God (1:17, 76; 3:4–6) or as the forerunner of Israel (7:27; cf. Exod. 23:20).

In Luke's view, John is the Spirit-filled "prophet of God" (1:15, 17, 76, 80) who is also "more than a prophet" (7:26). Even as he closes out the time of prophecy (16:16), he inaugurates the time of salvation (1:77; 3:6). He is the end-time figure of whom God says in scripture: "Behold, I send my messenger before you [Israel], who shall prepare your [Israel's] way before you [Israel]" (7:27; cf. Exod. 23:20). To perform this task, John appears in the desert region about the Jordan "proclaiming a baptism of repentance for the forgiveness of sins" (3:2–3; cf. 1:77). Although the Pharisees and the lawyers refuse to be baptized by him (7:30), the crowds, tax-collectors, and soldiers give ear to him (3:10–14; 7:29). In this way, he turns "many of the sons of Israel to the Lord their God" and readies "for the Lord [God] a people prepared" (1:16–17; Acts 13:24).

Toward the end of his ministry, John explicitly discounts the popular notion that he himself might be the Messiah (3:15). He directs the people away from himself toward the coming of one who is mightier than he (3:16). This Mightier One who is in fact the Messiah is, of course, Jesus, the royal Son of God, as the pericopes on the baptism (3:21–22), the genealogy (3:23–38), and the temptation (4:1–13) reveal. To mark the beginning of his public ministry in Israel, Luke has Jesus return from Jerusalem to Galilee and teach in the synagogues to the acclaim of all (4:14–15). As a part of this activity, Jesus also arrives in Nazareth, where he grew up, and attends the synagogue service on the sabbath (4:16). Under the pen of Luke, this narrative of Jesus' visit to the synagogue of Nazareth becomes in effect a programmatic statement on the nature and course of Jesus' entire ministry to Israel.[12]

The centerpiece of this narrative is the reading Jesus gives from Isaiah (4:18–19; cf. Isa. 58:6; 61:1–2). In this reading, Jesus designates himself as the one whom God has "anointed" with his "Spirit" (4:18). As is plain, the term "anointed" and "Spirit" allude to Jesus as the Messiah (Anointed One), the beloved Son whom God empowered following his baptism with the Holy Spirit (3:15–16, 22; 4:1, 14). Earlier, however, Luke showed that Jesus Son of God is also the Servant of God: in the temple, the "boy" ("servant") Jesus was found devoting himself to his Father's business (2:43, 49). Here in the synagogue of Nazareth as well, Jesus is about his Father's business. In the ministry he imputes to himself as he reads from Isaiah, he brings prophecy to fulfillment. Obediently, he places himself under the divine necessity (Greek: *dei*) to carry out God's plan of salvation (2:49; 4:43; 9:22; 13:33; 17:25; 22:37; 24:7, 26, 44). In so doing, he, the Messiah Son of God, stands forth as the Servant of God (cf. Acts 4:27).

Jesus, the Spirit-endowed Son and Servant of God, characterizes his ministry as one of "proclamation" (4:18–19). His powerful word announces good news on the one hand and accomplishes mighty acts on the other. "Word and work," therefore, become Luke's thumbnail description of the public activity of Jesus: he is a "prophet mighty in deed and word before God and all the people" (24:19; cf. Acts 1:1).

Specifically, Jesus declares in the synagogue at Nazareth that he has been commissioned by God to "announce good news to the poor" (4:18). The "poor" in Luke's thinking are, to be sure, the economically impoverished (14:13; 16:20; 19:8; 21:3). But what is distinctive about them is that they in their need look to God for help and receive with joy the promise of his end-time kingdom (6:20; 7:21–22). More broadly, the "poor" also symbolize the outcasts and the disenfranchised in Israel, those for whom the Lucan Jesus shows special concern in his ministry: women, children, tax-collectors, sinners, and the sick (cf. concordance). As Luke's Jesus says of himself, he has come "to seek and to save the lost" (19:10).

Jesus furthermore announces to the synagogue worshipers that he has been sent "to proclaim release to the captives and recovery of sight to the blind, and to set at liberty those who are oppressed" (4:18). The phrase to proclaim "recovery of sight to the blind" is a pointed reference to the healing activity of Jesus (cf. 7:21–22; 18:35–43). Behind the notions of "release to the captives" and "setting at liberty those who are oppressed" is the basic Lucan belief that the coming of Jesus means freedom from bondage to Satan and to sin. Jesus has already demonstrated his mastery over Satan in the pericope on the temptation (4:1–13; cf. 10:18; 11:14–22; 13:16). The outcome of all he undertakes is that "repentance for the forgiveness of sins might be proclaimed in his name" (24:47; cf. 5:20–24; 7:48; 11:4; 17:3–4).

In the final line of his reading, Jesus sums up the intent of his public ministry: "to proclaim the acceptable year of the Lord" (4:19). The allusion here is to the "year of jubilee" commanded by God in the law, when slaves were set free and debts abolished (Lev. 25:10). Jesus' mention of it amounts to a blanket announcement of the arrival of the time of salvation. Indeed, in a homiletical remark he appends to his reading, Jesus emphasizes this thought even more: "Today," he exclaims, "this scripture has been fulfilled in your hearing!" The theme that "today is the time of salvation" is typical of Luke and dots the pages of his Gospel (cf. esp. 2:11; 19:9; 23:43).

Jesus' words to the townspeople of Nazareth constitute a bold declaration of salvation. He has in effect heralded his presence in their midst as the presence of the Savior, who proffers them eschatological freedom and well-being (cf. 2:11). Their response to Jesus should have been: "Is this not the Son of God?" (cf. 3:22, 38; 4:3, 9, 34, 41).[13] Instead, they ask, "Is this not the son of Joseph?" (4:22; cf. 3:23). Accordingly, their perception of Jesus' person and message misses the mark, and Jesus takes them to task for their repudiation of him (4:23-24).

Nor is this all. Jesus also leaves Nazareth for Capernaum (4:31), never to return. Thus, he sets out already on the journey that takes him in and around Galilee (4:14—9:50) and then, in five stages, to Jerusalem (9:51—19:44). In fact, in the longer view of Luke, this journey to Jerusalem that Jesus even now begins will later be succeeded by yet another journey, that of his church to the Gentiles (4:25-27; Acts 1:8).

As Jesus travels toward Jerusalem, the ministry of word and work he ascribes to himself in Nazareth assumes the form of teaching, preaching, and healing (cf. 4:14-15, 43-44; 6:17-19). Through his ministry, he summons Israel to repentance (7:22-23; 11:32). His words to some are his message to all: "I have come to call . . . sinners to repentance" (5:32); or again, "I say to you, unless you repent, you will all . . . perish" (13:3, 5). Those who hear his call become his followers (cf. 5:27-28; 9:23, 59; 18:28). They constitute the restored Israel of God which receives the Messiah—King God has sent it (1:31-33, 68-75; 2:26; 9:20; 19:37-38). Thus, through his public ministry Jesus proffers to the whole of Israel the salvation he has initially proffered to the townspeople of Nazareth.

One last item calls for comment: Does Luke "divinize" the person of Jesus as he depicts him carrying out his public ministry to the degree that Matthew does? Interestingly, Luke seems to be more reserved on this score than Matthew. Take, for example, the term "Father." While the Lucan Jesus utters it at key moments during his ministry, the idiom "my Father," which occurs numerous times in Matthew's Gospel, occurs only three times in Luke's (10:22; 22:29; 24:49). Again, Luke does not divest Jesus of emotions to the extent Matthew does. Both Matthew and Luke picture Jesus as "being amazed" (Luke 7:9) and "having compassion" (Luke 7:13). Like Matthew, Luke also does not attribute to Jesus "anger" (Mark 3:5), "indignation" (Mark 10:14), or "love" for a man (Mark 10:21).

But unlike Matthew, Luke does say that Jesus "weeps" (19:41) and calls his disciples "my friends" (12:4). And finally, while persons certainly show Jesus respect in Luke's Gospel and pay him homage, it is not said that he is "worshiped" (*proskynein*) until after the resurrection (24:52), and the disciples do not uniformly address him as "Lord." Of the synoptic evangelists and the writers of Q, Matthew appears to have "spiritualized" the figure of the earthly Jesus the most.

Jesus' Ministry of Preaching and Teaching

Central to Jesus' preaching in Luke's story is the kingdom, or rule, of God. It is no different, of course, in Q, Mark, or Matthew. But nowhere does Luke provide a summary of Jesus' message of the kingdom (cf. Mark 1:14–15; Matt. 4:17). On the contrary, he simply writes *that* Jesus proclaims the kingdom of God (4:43; 8:1; 9:11). Such bare notations suffice, however, because Jesus' "sermon" in Nazareth is in essence Luke's explication of Jesus' message of the kingdom: in Jesus Messiah himself, in his words and deeds, God is present with his end-time rule (4:18–19; cf. 1:31–33; 19:38; Acts 8:12; 28:23, 31).

Accordingly, in Jesus Messiah, the Son and Servant of God, the kingdom of God is a present reality. "But if it is by the finger of God that I cast out demons," declares Jesus, "then the kingdom of God has come upon you!" (11:20). Still, although the rule of God is present in Jesus, it cannot be perceived except by those to whom "it is given" (8:10); hence, the rule of God is a hidden reality. Jesus touches on this truth in his reply to a Pharisee who asks him when the kingdom of God will come; he answers, "The kingdom of God does not come with signs to be observed; nor will they say, 'Lo, here it is!' or 'There!' for behold, the kingdom of God is in the midst of you" (17:20–21).

As a reality that remains hidden in the present, the kingdom of God will be consummated in splendor in the future. In keeping with Christian tradition, Luke, too, associates the glorious appearance of God's eschatological kingdom with the sudden revelation from heaven of Jesus Son of man (9:26–27; 21:27–31). Moreover, Luke also affirms that the magnificent kingdom of the future is continuous with the hidden kingdom of the present: whether now as Messiah—

Lord or then as the transcendent Son of man, God exercises his end-time rule through Jesus (13:18–19, 20–21).

Compared with the other synoptics or Q, the problematic of the delay of the final appearance of Jesus and of the kingdom is most acute in Luke's Gospel (cf. 17:20; 19:11; Acts 1:6). Luke meets the difficulties this delay has spawned chiefly in two ways. On the one hand, because the coming of God's splendid kingdom has already been delayed, Luke can assure the members of his community that this event is necessarily that much closer: "But I tell you truly, there are some standing here," asserts the Lucan Jesus, "who will not taste of death before they see the kingdom of God" (9:27). And on the other hand, Luke enjoins the members of his community to concentrate their energies, not on calculating the time of the parousia as such (17:20–24), but on the matters that count most: faithfulness (12:42–48; 19:11–27), watchfulness (12:35–40), diligence in prayer (18:1), and perseverance in faith (17:5–6, 22; 18:8).

If preaching is one major aspect of Jesus' public ministry, teaching is another. Indeed, in Luke's story as in Mark's and Matthew's, teaching seems to be the principal activity of the earthly Jesus. Thus, Luke's own summary of his Gospel is that it tells of "all that Jesus began both to do and to teach" (Acts 1:1). And only in Luke's version of the passion does the Sanhedrin urge Pilate to indict Jesus specifically for his "teaching": "He stirs up the people, teaching throughout all Judea, from Galilee even to this place" (23:5; cf. 4:15; 13:22; 19:47–48; 21:37–38).

As the Son and Servant of God anointed with the Spirit (3:22; 4:18), Jesus teaches in Israel with the same divine authority with which he preaches (4:31–32; 20:1–2). What he teaches is the "way [will] of God" (20:21). As his enemies ironically acknowledge, his word is recognized in Israel as being right, impartial, and true (20:21); it elicits wonder even from them (20:26). In Luke's mind, then, Jesus is the authoritative teacher of Israel (9:35), the one who is utterly "orthodox" ("right") in his exposition of the will of God (20:21; cf. 20:1–8).

To teach the will of God, however, is for Luke not different from teaching the "law of the Lord [God]" (2:23–24, 39; 10:26; 16:17). And the law of the Lord, of course, is one with the "law of Moses" (cf. 2:23 to 2:22). As the authoritative teacher of Israel, therefore, the Lucan Jesus is also the "orthodox" teacher of the law of Moses (20:21–22).[14]

Mark and especially Matthew do not shrink from portraying Jesus as revising the law of Moses even as he expounds it. By contrast, Luke is much more circumspect on this score. In his eyes, the Jewish allegation that Jesus is out to "change the customs [law] which Moses delivered to us [Israel]" is without foundation (cf. Acts 6:13–14). Quite the opposite, Luke insists that Jesus should rather be seen to be the faithful advocate of the law of Moses.

The infancy narratives already reflect this point of view. For one thing, the infants John and Jesus are both surrounded by persons whose piety is exemplary. What is said of Zechariah and Elizabeth could, in fact, be said of all of them—Mary and Joseph (1:38; 2:22), the shepherds (2:15–16), Simeon (2:25), and Anna (2:37): "And they were . . . righteous before God, walking in all the commandments and ordinances of the Lord blameless" (1:6). For another thing, after Jesus is born, every care is taken so that the ritual requirements of the Mosaic law might be scrupulously observed: Jesus is circumcised, he is given his name, purification is made, he is presented to the Lord, and sacrifice is offered (2:21–24). And last, the infancy narratives close by alluding to Jesus' own ministry of teaching the law when they place him, as a twelve-year-old, in the temple sitting amidst the "teachers" of Israel and recount of him: "And all who heard him were amazed at his understanding and his answers" (2:46–47).

Once he has begun his public ministry of teaching, the Lucan Jesus staunchly upholds the law of Moses. "But it is easier for heaven and earth to pass away," he declares, "than for one serif of the law to fall" (16:17). Moreover, he likewise contends for the validity of the whole law in the sense that he does not reduce it to the core-element of "love" (cf. 10:25–28 with Mark 12:28–34 and Matt. 22:34–40). To be sure, he (or his disciples) is attacked by the Pharisees no fewer than four times for allegedly violating the sabbath rest (6:1–5, 6–11; 13:10–17; 14:1–6; Exod. 20:8–11; Deut. 5:12–15). Jesus' defense, however, is that it is precisely the doing of God's will that has impelled him to act as he has (cf. 13:16: "Was it not necessary . . ."). And by the same token, Jesus also sharpens certain of the Mosaic commandments, such as those on divorce

(16:18; Deut. 24:1), retribution,[15] and love of one's enemies (6:27–28, 32–35; Lev. 19:18). Still, the issue in these cases is plainly that of intensification, not abrogation.

Although the Jesus of Luke is clearly the orthodox teacher of the law of Moses, the attitude he assumes toward the tradition of the elders, i.e., the oral law promulgated by the Pharisees, is less apparent. Invited by a Pharisee to dine with him, Jesus astonishes his host by not ritually washing his hands before dinner (11:37–38). This suggests that Luke's Jesus does not strictly adhere to the code of the Pharisees.

But there are other indications that point in the opposite direction. In his woes against the Pharisees, Jesus says of their tithing mint and rue and every herb that this ought not to be "neglected" (11:42). In his woes against the lawyers, he tacitly grants that they have possession of the "key of knowledge" (11:52). On another level, there is also no disparagement in Luke's Gospel of the tradition of the elders such as there is, for example, in Mark's: "You leave the commandment of God, and hold fast the tradition of men" (Mark 7:8). And if the figure of Paul in Acts can be of any value in helping one form a picture of Luke's Jesus, it cannot be overlooked that Paul stands forth as a "Pharisee" (Acts 23:6; 26:5) whose fealty to the "law of our fathers" (Acts 22:3), to the "God of our fathers" (Acts 24:14), and to the "customs of our fathers" (Acts 28:17) can in no wise be impugned.

If the weight of the evidence seems to imply that the Lucan Jesus is to be thought of as upholding both the Mosaic law and the traditions, this does not mean that he therefore escapes conflict with the Jewish leaders. In Luke's story as in Q, Mark, and Matthew, Jesus becomes embroiled in debate with them. Representative of such debate is the section 11:37–52, where Jesus pronounces two series of three woes each against the Pharisees and the lawyers, or scribes. Jesus' underlying contention is that the Jewish leaders do not do the will of God (cf. 11:28: "hear the word of God and keep it"; also 12:1; Acts 7:53; 23:3). He charges that they hide "rapacity" and "wickedness" behind a noble front (11:39), and condemns them for all of the following. They are neglectful of the law's demand of justice for the neighbor and of love for God (11:42). They revel in the fawning adulation of public recognition (11:43). Inwardly unclean, they make others who associate with them unclean (11:44). While insisting that people must observe a panoply of rules and regulations, they do nothing to show them how (11:46). They are like their fathers, for the only prophets who appeal to them are dead prophets whose word they have "neutralized" (11:47–48). And although they possess the key of the knowledge of God's will, they have not availed themselves of such knowledge to please God and have prevented others from attaining to it (11:52).

Within the flow of Luke's story, the upshot of Jesus' clash with the leaders of the Jews is that they become exceedingly hostile toward him (11:53; cf. 6:11). In fact, their hostility marks them as the ones who will look for a way to have Jesus put to death (22:2).

Jesus' Ministry of Healing

Luke conceives of Jesus' public ministry, we said, as one of word and work (24:19). Not only does Jesus preach and teach, therefore, but he also performs miraculous deeds.

In Luke's scheme of things, Jesus, the Son and Servant of God, derives the "power" (*dynamis*) to perform miraculous deeds, and the "authority" (*exousia*) to command such power, through his anointing with the Holy Spirit (3:22; 4:17; Acts 10:38). As in Mark and Matthew, his miraculous deeds include healing diseases (7:21–22), raising the dead (7:11–17; 8:40–42, 51–56), exorcising demons (4:36; 6:18; 11:20), and controlling the forces of nature (cf. 8:22–25). Still, to a greater degree than the Matthaean if not the Marcan Jesus, the Jesus of Luke strikes the posture of the popular miracle-worker. He is pictured as "charged" with supernatural power, so that a whole crowd, for example, needs only to touch him for healing to take place (6:19; 5:17; but cf. 8:44–46 to Mark 5:27–31). Moreover, whereas Mark and Matthew distinguish between the "mighty acts" (*dynameis*) Jesus does and the "signs and wonders" (*sēmeia kai terata*) the false prophets do (Mark 13:22; Matt. 24:24), Luke rather massively ascribes all such miraculous feats to Jesus himself ("Jesus of Nazareth, a man attested to . . . by mighty works and wonders and signs" [Acts 2:22]).

It is not simply "delight in the miraculous," however, that prompts Luke to enlarge his portrait of Jesus as miracle-worker. He does so in order to show how bounteous are the blessings which God in his mercy showers on Israel through his Son and Servant Jesus (Acts 2:22; 10:38). In Jesus, God is present with his end-time rule to engage Satan in cosmic struggle. Satan, too, has a kingdom (11:18) and even claims, in fact, that he has been installed as lord over the whole of the inhabited world (4:5–6). His kingdom, however, is one of darkness (22:53; Acts 26:18), populated by demons (cf. 11:17–20). He takes possession of people, and illness is a sign that one has fallen victim to him (13:16). Among the disciples, Judas comes under his sway (22:3), and it is only the prayers of Jesus which protect Peter from the same fate (22:31–32). Indeed, any person who would hear the message of salvation and come to faith is open to attack by Satan (8:12).

Still, Jesus Son of God is stronger than the "strong man" Satan (4:1–13; 11:21–22). Through his ministry of healing, Jesus rescues people from Satan's dominion (10:18) and enables them to enter the sphere where God reigns (11:20; 13:16). Consequently, with his ministry of healing Jesus "lays waste" the kingdom of Satan (11:17). What is more, he also summons all of Israel to perceive the significance of his powerful acts and to repent and to be saved (cf. 10:13; 19:37–40).

Jesus' Passion and Exaltation

In telling of Jesus' ministry to Israel, Luke devotes the first main part of his story to Jesus' activity in Galilee (4:14—9:50) and the second main part to his journey in five stages to Jerusalem (9:51—19:44). Once Jesus has reached Jerusalem, Luke focuses first on his teaching in the temple (19:45—21:38) and then on his passion, death, resurrection, and ascension (22:1—24:53).

Luke recasts the pericope on the triumphal entry so that it is not said that Jesus enters Jerusalem (cf. Mark 11:11) but the temple (19:45). As Israel's King and God's Son and Servant (19:38), Jesus reclaims his Father's house (2:46–49) for its proper purpose: the worship of God (19:46) and therefore also the teaching of his will (19:47–48).

Having reclaimed the temple, Jesus instructs the people daily, and they hang on his words (19:47–48; 21:37–38). By contrast, the leaders of the Jews plot his destruction and endeavor to trap him in debate (19:47; 20:1—21:4). Jesus concludes his teaching with a lengthy discourse on the last things (21:5–36). Because the pass-over is now at hand (22:1), Luke begins his account of the passion. The following points characterize this account.

The most noteworthy feature of Luke's version of the passion is his repeated insistence that the suffering of Jesus takes place in ac-cordance with God's predetermined plan of salvation. Jesus dies in Luke's Gospel as the Messiah—King, the Son of God (22:66–71; 23:38). As such, he has full knowledge of God's plan for him and predicts his suffering (9:22; 13:33; 17:25; 22:37; cf. 9:44; 18:31–33). By the same token, he likewise willingly and obediently takes it upon himself to carry out this plan (9:51; 13:33; 17:25; 22:37, 42). In addition, since his passion predictions remain incompre-hensible to his disciples (9:45; 18:34; 22:24, 38), he will also, following Easter, open their minds to understand that his suffering had long before been foretold in OT scripture (24:6–8, 25–27, 44–45). In all, therefore, Luke records that Jesus makes some seven references to the divine necessity (*dei*) of his suffering (9:22; 13:33; 17:25; 22:37; 24:7, 26, 44). By comparison, the Marcan Jesus makes but one such reference (8:31). Why is Luke so concerned to stress this theme? Because it gives answer to the fundamental ques-tion as to why the Messiah must die. He must die because God has ordained it.

Another distinctive feature of Luke's presentation of the passion is that he construes the suffering of Jesus as a struggle with Satan. The way to the cross is a "temptation" Jesus must endure (22:28), and when his captors come to take him, he says ominously, "But this is your hour, and the power of darkness" (22:53). From one standpoint, therefore, it is Satan who has the leaders of the Jews at his command (22:52–53), just as it is also Satan who leads Judas to betray Jesus (22:3–4) and Peter to deny him (22:31–34).

But Satan's involvement does not mean that the human agents who plot Jesus' death and bring it about are consequently guiltless (22:22). The blame for this Luke lays squarely at the feet of the leaders of the Jews (chaps. 22—23). In fact, Luke tends to mini-mize the role that both Pilate and the Jewish people play in Jesus' condemnation. To be sure, Pilate is guilty of complicity (23:24), and the people call for Jesus to be crucified (23:13, 21). But by the same token Pilate also tries repeatedly to get Jesus freed (23:16, 20, 22), and at the scene beneath the cross the people do not mock Jesus but only stand by and watch (23:35; cf. 23:48).

The charge the leaders of the Jews bring against Jesus is sedition against Rome: "We found this man misleading our nation, and forbidding us to give tribute to Caesar, and saying that he himself is Christ a king" (23:2; cf. 23:5). Luke sees to it that this charge is debunked and that Jesus stands forth as the righteous martyr who incurs the fate of all God's prophets (11:47–51; 13:33–34; 24:19–20). Thus, Pilate asserts three times that Jesus is innocent of any crime (23:4, 13–14, 22), and claims that Herod is of the same mind (23:15). The dying criminal likewise attests to his innocence (23:40–41), and upon Jesus' death, the centurion declares him to be "righteous" (23:47), which in Luke's vocabulary means that his has been a life well-pleasing to God (cf. 1:6; Acts 3:14; 10:22).

Ironically, there is one aspect of the Jewish charge against Jesus which is true: Jesus is in fact "a king" (cf. 23:2 to 19:38). For Luke, however, Jesus is King, not as one who wields political power, but as one who serves (22:27). Moreover, the service he renders is the gift of salvation he bestows (19:10). This comes to the fore in the exchange he has on the cross with the one criminal. To the plea, "Jesus, remember me when you come into your kingdom," Jesus replies, "Truly I say to you, today you will be with me in paradise!" (23:42–43). To one who repents, Jesus, the King, grants access to the kingdom of God.

Finally, what does Luke make of Jesus' death, resurrection, and ascension? In Mark and Matthew, Jesus' death on the cross atones for sin. Since Luke has his own conception of salvation, which we shall discuss shortly, he does not interpret the cross in this way. Instead, Luke describes the cross as the divinely necessitated humiliation of Jesus (22:37; Acts 8:32–33), the resurrection as his vindication by God that he is indeed his Messiah (20:17–18; Acts 4:10–12), and the ascension as his entrance into the heavenly glory of divine rule (24:26, 51; cf. 20:42–43; 22:69). At the same time, Luke also views all of these events together, in which case Jesus' death, resurrection, and ascension represent his "exodus" (9:31) or "ascension" (9:51) from suffering into heavenly glory (24:26).

DISCIPLESHIP

The goal Luke pursues with his gospel story is to show that in Jesus Messiah, his Son and Servant, God proffers salvation to Israel. In surrounding himself with disciples, therefore, the Lucan Jesus is not founding the church as such; this takes place at Pentecost (24: 49; Acts 2:1–4). Instead, as Israel's Messiah, Jesus is beginning the process of gathering to himself the true Israel.[16]

Because Jesus Messiah gathers the true Israel, the whole of his ministry, from its beginning to the crucifixion, has as its setting the broad public of Israel (cf. 4:14–15, 44; 23:5). In sharp contrast to Mark and Matthew, Luke almost never pictures Jesus as teaching in private (Mark 4:33–34; Matt. 13:36). Neither does Luke permit him to travel in the Gentile regions of Tyre, Sidon, or the Decapolis (Mark 7:24, 31; Matt. 15:21). Rather, it is squarely in the midst of Israel that Jesus is active, and a passage such as the following illustrates this well: "In the meantime, when so many thousands of the multitude had gathered together that they trod upon one another, he began to say . . ." (12:1).

Accordingly, Jesus gathers his disciples from the wide populace of Israel, and they constitute the true Israel (9:23; 14:25–27). The people he summons are a diverse lot: fishermen (5:1–11), tax-collectors and sinners (5:27–28, 32; 15:1), common persons (9:23; 14:25–27), a certain man (9:59), a rich ruler (18:18, 22), and a chief tax-collector (19:1–10). In addition, he is also accompanied by a large group of women (8:2–3), who also seem to be his disciples (23:55—24:11). In all, those about Jesus are thought of by Luke as comprising a substantial number. This is clear from 10:1, where Jesus dispatches no fewer than seventy disciples on a missionary journey, and from the fact that Luke terms the disciples of Jesus a "great crowd" (6:17) in one instance and a "whole throng" in another (19:37).

Because the adherents of Jesus do not stand apart from Israel, Luke does little of a terminological nature in his Gospel to single them out as a special community. Thus, he calls them neither the "church" (cf. Acts 9:31, etc.) nor "the Way" (Acts 9:2; 19:9, 23; 22:4, 14, 22). To be sure, Luke designates their inner circle as the "twelve," but this term itself alludes to Israel (22:30). In general, just as John and the Pharisees have "disciples" (5:33; 7:18; 11:1), so Luke regularly refers to Jesus' adherents as his "disciples" ("learners"). The disciples of Jesus are those who have heard his authoritative summons and have "followed" after him (5:27; 9:23, 59; 18:28). As they have done so, he has become their "Lord"[17] and "Master,"[18] God has become their "Father" (11:2; 12:32), and they have become "brothers" of one another (6:42; 8:21; 17:3).

Following after Jesus, the disciples live in the sphere of God's end-time rule (6:20–23; 12:32; 17:21). Indeed, they are people of a particular kind. As the beatitudes describe them, they are the "poor," the "hungry," the "weeping," and the "persecuted," i.e., people who pin their hopes on God alone and look to him for fullness, joy, and vindication (6:20–23). They are also the kind of people who will "leave behind everything," including home, family, and possessions, in order to be with Jesus (5:11, 28; 9:23, 59–60; 14:25–27; 18:28). In short, they are the kind of people who "seek first God's kingdom" against that day when the Son of man shall be revealed from heaven to "redeem" them (17:30; 21:27–28).

The role of the disciples in Luke's story is multiple. For one thing, they are, as the constant companions of Jesus, witnesses to his ministry of word and deed (Acts 1:21–22). Hence, they are the guarantors of the Jesus tradition in the time of the church following his ascension. For another thing, they engage in missionary activity. In 9:1–6, Jesus empowers the twelve to preach and to heal in the villages of Galilee. Their activity thus becomes an extension of his own. In 10:1–16, Jesus, on his way to Jerusalem, sends out the seventy disciples to heal and to proclaim the kingdom in all the cities and localities through which he is about to pass. Hence, their ministry, too, becomes an extension of his.

In the third place, the disciples serve as a link between the earthly ministry of Jesus and the ministry of the post-Pentecost church. The twelve (eleven), for example, do not abandon Jesus in Luke's story but remain with him even in the trials of his suffering (22:28). Moreover, after his resurrection Jesus appears to Peter, the eleven, and to the other disciples (24:30–31, 33–53). At these appearances, he opens their minds to understand that both his earthly ministry and their future ministry have been ordained by God and foretold in the scriptures (24:25–27, 44–47). In this way, he makes of them witnesses to his resurrection and also prepares them for the events surrounding Pentecost and their ministry to follow (24:48–49, 50–53).

A word on the "twelve" is perhaps in order. Matthew seems to equate the disciples of Jesus with the twelve (9:37; 10:1). Luke manifestly does not. For him, the twelve are first of all the "apostles" (6:13) whose number attests to the fact that the disciples constitute the true Israel (22:30). They form the "inner circle" of the larger body of disciples in the Gospel and serve as the leaders of the Christian community that is described in the early chapters of Acts.

SOTERIOLOGY

Luke wrote his Gospel about A.D. 85 for Greek-speaking Christians of both Jewish and Gentile origin who were at home in an urban setting, perhaps in Syria or Asia Minor. In conclusion of our study, we ask about the nature of this community and its understanding of salvation.

The Community of Luke

Luke speaks pointedly of the "desolation" of Jerusalem (21:20–24; cf. 13:34–35; 23:28–31). He has also made use of Mark as one of his sources (cf. 1:1–4). Consequently, there is good reason to suppose that the date for Luke's Gospel is about A.D. 85.

The constituency of this community is both Jewish and Gentile in background. This is evident from the book of Acts. In depicting large-scale conversions of Jews and Gentiles to Christianity, Luke hints at the composition of his own church (cf., e.g., 2:41; 4:4; 6:7; 11:20–21; 13:43; 14:1; 17:4; 18:8). In addition, the purpose of the agreement James dictates in Acts 15:20 is precisely to enable Gentile Christians to live in fellowship with Jewish Christians. We can assume that this agreement was in force in Luke's day.

The Lucan community also seems to be urban in character and contains within it people of diverse socioeconomic strata. A simple statistic must suffice to elucidate the first point: whereas Luke employs the word "village" only thirteen times in the Gospel and Acts, he employs the word "city" eighty-one times (39× + 42×). It would appear that Luke, as opposed to Mark, for example, overwhelmingly makes the "city" the setting for the events about which he narrates exactly because his own community is an urban one.

Luke's preoccupation with the theme of "riches"[19] suggests that his community is economically heterogeneous. The membership embraces both the rich and the poor (cf. 6:20, 24; 7:22; 12:16–21; 14:21; 18:24–27; 19:1–19). Indeed, one of Luke's principal concerns is how the rich relate to the poor. On this score, he contends that the possession of wealth is neither a sign of God's favor (12:15; 16:13–15) nor in and of itself evil (18:24–27; 19:1–10). The problem is that it entices one to serve the self instead of the neighbor and God (8:14; 12:16–34; 16:13, 19–31). Hence, the disciple must be prepared at any time to renounce it (14:33). In fact, to counter the negative influence of their wealth, there are two things the rich must do. The one is to give alms, for thus they are observing the will of God (12:31–34; Acts 9:36; 10:2, 4, 31). The other is to imitate the practice of the early church, where the rich gave of their abundance so that the poor did not go without (Acts 2:44–45; 4:32–35).

The organizational makeup of the Lucan community is not immediately discernible. The "apostles" are figures of the past, and it is not clear that the office entrusted "the seven" (Acts 6:1–6) ever became permanent. More to the point perhaps are Luke's references in Acts to "prophets." They not only foretell the future (11:27–28; 21:10–11) but also seem to be missionaries and teachers (13:1–3; 15:32). Barnabas and Saul (Paul), for instance, are among their number (Acts 13:1–3). In any case, Luke's own community almost certainly has within it both teachers (1:4) and missionaries (cf. 11:49; 24:47; Acts 1:8). Moreover, if Acts 14:23 and 20:17 are any clue, it may also be that Luke's community is supervised by elders, or presbyters. Their task is to oversee both the faith and life of the community (Acts 20:28–30). Still, this suggestion must remain tentative.

Socioculturally, the Lucan community lived in an area where the Jewish and Gentile populations were both strong and were both subjecting it to harassment and persecution. The situation of these Christians is aptly described in Acts 14:22, where Paul and Barnabas say, ". . . through many tribulations we must enter the kingdom of God." A survey of the Gospel alone reveals that the Lucan Christians have endured, or must endure, such afflictions as the following: the hatred of others (6:22, 27; 21:17); social ostracism, including exclusion from the synagogue and the cursing of one's name associated with this (6:22); verbal abuse of various kinds (6:22, 28); arrest by the authorities as a result of one's own family bringing charges against one (21:16); judicial harassment, such as being flogged in the synagogue or jailed or hauled before Gentile authorities (21:12); and even death (11:49).

Other problems, too, attend the situation in which these Christians find themselves. In the Gospel, three such problems are especially apparent.[20] For one thing, there are those who are unable to hold to the Christian way and who surrender their faith and become apostate (8:13; 18:8). For another, there are likewise those who, although they do not fall away, nevertheless long for the revelation from heaven of Jesus Son of man (17:22, 30) and wonder why the kingdom of God has not yet appeared in splendor (17:20–21; 19:11). To these Christians Luke explains that the eschatological kingdom is a present as well as a future reality (11:20; 17:21), and that just as Jesus made many predictions (e.g., about his suffering, death, resurrection, ascension, the destruction of Jerusalem, and the future ministry of his disciples) which have all come to pass, so they can rest assured that he will honor the promises he has made to his church about the end-times and his final coming (cf. 21:8–36). And last, there are furthermore those who ask why, if Jesus is the Messiah, he has seemingly been repudiated by Israel? To these Christians Luke's reply is that it is the church, in fact, who is the true Israel, in whose heritage the Gentiles share (2:30–32; 24:47), and that those Jews who willfully repudiate Jesus remove themselves from the chosen people of God.

The Locus of Salvation

To meet the needs of his community, Luke has written a kerygmatic story that, in terms of his Gospel, tells of Jesus Messiah, the Son and Servant of God, from his birth to his ascension. It is this word about Jesus, proclaimed by the church, that is to Luke's way of thinking the word of salvation (Acts 4:12; 13:26).

In the speeches of Acts, Luke provides us with an anatomy of his understanding of salvation (cf. 2:14–39; 3:12–26; 4:9–12; 5:30–

32; 10:34–43; 13:16–38). Indeed, these speeches are a retelling in miniature of his Gospel. In them, God is proclaimed as the author of salvation, who in faithfulness to his promises to Israel has sent Jesus as Savior. In the power of the Holy Spirit Jesus, preceded by John, has discharged a ministry of word and mighty deed, releasing people from the tyranny of Satan. In ignorance but also in accordance with divine purpose, Israel itself had Pilate put Jesus to death. Nonetheless, God has raised him from the dead, thus showing that he is in truth the Messiah, and he, in turn, has appeared to his disciples. Moreover, God has also exalted him to lordship and has ordained that he shall be the Judge of all at the end of time.

Luke affirms that in this word about Jesus, God graciously reaches out to people of every nation. It is his will that people believe it, repent of sin, and submit to baptism. Those who do so respond receive the forgiveness of sins and the gift of the Holy Spirit. In addition, they also become members of the church, which is the community of the saved.

For Luke, therefore, it is in the proclamation of the word of salvation as just sketched and in joining the church that one finds the locus of salvation. Hence, in contrast to Q, which focuses on the parousia, and to Mark's Gospel, which focuses on the cross, Luke makes the whole of Jesus' life—birth, ministry, suffering, death, resurrection, ascension, and parousia—the object of proclamation. One result of this is that Luke, compared with Mark, interprets the Lord's supper quite differently. If the passage 22:19b–20 is set aside as textually uncertain and the passage 22:14–19a is accepted as the Lucan text, the Lord's supper ceases to be a commemoration of the atonement. Instead, it becomes an anticipation of the messianic banquet that Jesus will celebrate with his own in the consummated kingdom of God.

The mission the resurrected Jesus has given the church of Luke is that of proclaiming repentance and the forgiveness of sins in his name to all the nations (24:47; Acts 1:8). It is probable that Luke's church is also still engaged in a mission to the Jews (Acts 28:24, 30–31). However that may be, this church presses forward in its task only in the face of internal problems and persecution. With this situation squarely in view, Luke has written his gospel-story in order to give the Christians of his church (and Theophilus) a clear and compelling account of what God has accomplished for their salvation in Jesus Messiah. In telling this gospel-story, Luke attests to the faithfulness of God in keeping his promises, to the Lordship of Jesus Messiah, God's Son and their Savior, and to the sustaining and guiding power of God's Holy Spirit. Correspondingly, he enjoins his fellow Christians to master the future through increased faith (17:5–6; 18:8), through perseverence in hardship (8:15; 21: 19), through diligence in prayer (11:1–4; 18:1; 21:36), and through a lively hope in their ultimate redemption by Jesus Son of man at the latter day (21:27–28). In short, Luke exhorts them to take up their cross daily and to follow after Jesus (9:23; 14:27).

NOTES

1. Cf. Luke 4:14–15, 44; 6:17; 7:17; 23:5.
2. Cf. W. C. Robinson, *Der Weg des Herrn* (TF 36; Hamburg-Bergstedt: Evangelischer Verlag, 1964), pp. 30–39.
3. On Luke's concept of "prophecy and fulfillment," cf. P. Schubert, "The Structure and Significance of Luke 24," *Neutestamentliche Studien für Rudolf Bultmann*, ed. W. Eltester (BZNW 21; Berlin: Alfred Töpelmann, 1954), pp. 165–86; P. S. Minear, "Luke's Use of the Birth Stories," *Studies in Luke–Acts*, eds. L. E. Keck and J. L. Martyn (reprint ed.; Philadelphia: Fortress, 1980), pp. 111–30.
4. Cf. G. Voss, *Die Christologie der lukanischen Schriften in Grundzügen* (StudNeot 2; Paris: Desclée de Brouwer, 1965), pp. 47–54.
5. On Luke's overall understanding of Jesus, cf. F. Danker, *Luke* (Proclamation Commentaries; Philadelphia: Fortress, 1976), pp. 18–43; E. Franklin, *Christ the Lord* (Philadelphia: Westminster, 1975), pp. 48–76.
6. Cf. J. A. Fitzmyer, "The Composition of Luke, Chapter 9," *Perspectives on Luke–Acts*, ed. C. H. Talbert (Perspectives in Religious Studies 5; Danville, Va.: Association of Baptist Professors of Religion, 1978), pp. 139–52.
7. Although at 5:24 Jesus refers to himself as the Son of man, this is not, strictly speaking, the answer Luke has in mind to the question, "Who is this?" If Son of man were in fact the answer, this answer would have been stated and there would be no reason for Luke to see to it that the question of Jesus' identity continues to be repeated, at 7:49; 8:25; 9:9, 18, 20. As we point out in the body of the chapter, the answer Luke is thinking of comes at 9:20.
8. Cf. Luke 17:22, 25; 18:8; 19:10; 21:36; 22:48; 24:7. Also G. Schneider, "'Der Menschensohn' in der lukanischen Christologie," *Jesus und der Menschensohn*, eds. R. Pesch and R. Schnackenburg (*Festschrift* A. Vögtle; Freiburg: Herder, 1975), pp. 267–82.
9. Incidentally, it is in this rather minimal form, namely, in the inability of the disciples to comprehend the passion predictions (9:45; 18:34), that Luke has taken over Mark's secret about the person of Jesus

(cf. W. Wrede, *The Messianic Secret,* tr. J. C. G. Greig [London: James Clarke, 1971], pp. 164–80).
  10. Cf. Luke 9:44; 18:32; 22:22, 48; 24:7.
  11. Cf. Luke 9:22; 17:25; 18:32–33.
  12. Cf. R. C. Tannehill, "The Mission of Jesus according to Luke," *Jesus in Nazareth,* ed. W. Eltester (BZNW 40; Berlin: Walter de Gruyter, 1972), pp. 51–75.
  13. Cf. F. W. Danker, *Jesus and the New Age* (reprint ed.; St. Louis: Clayton Publishing House, 1974), p. 59.
  14. Cf. J. Jervell, "The Law in Luke–Acts," *Luke and the People of God* (Minneapolis: Augsburg Publishing House, 1972), pp. 133–51.
  15. Luke 6:29–30; Exod. 21:23–25; Lev. 24:19–20; Deut. 19:19–20.
  16. Cf. G. Lohfink, *Die Sammlung Israels* (SANT 39; München: Kösel-Verlag, 1975), pp. 63–84.
  17. Cf. Luke 10:1, 17; 11:1.
  18. Luke 5:5; 8:24, 45; 9:33, 49; cf. 17:13.
  19. Cf. R. J. Karris, "Poor and Rich: The Lukan *Sitz im Leben*," *Perspectives on Luke–Acts,* ed. C. H. Talbert (Perspectives in Religious Studies 5; Danville, Va.: Association of Baptist Professors of Religion, 1978), pp. 112–25; L. T. Johnson, *The Literary Function of Possessions in Luke–Acts* (SBLDS 39; Missoula, Mont.: Scholars, 1977).
  20. For a broader discussion of the situation-in-life of Luke's community, cf. R. J. Karris, "Missionary Communities: A New Paradigm for the Study of Luke–Acts," *The Catholic Biblical Quarterly,* 41 (1979), 80–97; G. Krodel, *Acts* (Proclamation Commentaries; Philadelphia: Fortress, 1981).